The Practical House Officer

Dr. Keith E. Evans.

The Practical House Officer

I.A. Mitchell

BSc MB BS
Senior House Officer
Guy's Hospital
London

G.R. Teale

BSc MB BS
Senior House Officer
Queen Mary's University Hospital
London

Blackwell Special Projects
Oxford

© 1992 by
Blackwell Scientific Publications
(Blackwell Special Projects)
Editorial Office:
Osney Mead, Oxford OX2 0EL

First published 1992

Set by Times Graphics, Singapore
Printed and bound in Great Britain
by The Alden Press, Oxford

DISTRIBUTORS

Marston Book Services Ltd
PO Box 87
Oxford OX2 0DT
(*Orders:* Tel: 0865 791155
          Fax: 0865 791927
          Telex: 837515)

British Library
Cataloguing in Publication Data

Mitchell, I. A.
  The practical house officer
  I. Title II. Teale, G. R.
  610.6952

  ISBN 0-632-03309-6

Contents

3 Practical Procedures, 103

4 Surgical Considerations, 151

5 Cardiac Arrests, 155

6 Common Calls, 160

Foreword

How refreshing it is to be able to write the foreword to a book which combines so admirably compassion, good sense and practical advice. There are plenty of books guiding newly qualified house officers through the intricacies of handling medical emergencies, and many have found comfort in these. However over the years since I qualified (and there are now many of them), I have become increasingly aware of the stresses and strains imposed on young doctors by the rigours of present-day house jobs. Where, I have wondered, is the book to help them cope with the emotional, physical, intellectual and financial stress of their first job? Where is the book to guide them through the innumerable bureaucracies in which our health service is now entwined? Where is the book that emphasises the importance of communication, and gives empathetic advice on how to communicate with patients, bereaved relatives, health work colleagues and even the bank manager?

Drs Mitchell and Teale, with commendable lucidity and brevity, have written just the book that I have been looking for. I have learned much through reading it and I am sure that there are as many senior as junior doctors who will have good reason to thank them both for writing it. Mitchell and Teale talk about the efficient use of time, and the fact that they have managed to write this book so soon after qualification testifies to their efficient use of this, the most precious of nonrenewable commodities. It also confirms my view that this book is based on firm foundations.

I consider it a privilege to have been asked to write the foreword and anticipate that this book will get the wide readership that it deserves.

Robin Stott FRCP
Consultant Physician, Lewisham Hospital
Medical Director, Guy's and Lewisham Trust

Preface

The differences between life as a student and life as a junior doctor are immeasurable. No longer are you able to spend afternoons playing cricket or going window shopping; instead you are now a member of that infamous rat race. And what a rat race the hospital medical world is; from the flexible hours of a student's life to the endless compulsory hours as a house officer. Few find that they were adequately prepared for their new existence.

Suddenly you will be faced with situations which you have never experienced before and many will expect you to cope as if by magic. The sheer variety of your duties, the speed at which you will need to complete them and your general lack of experience and 'know-how' can rapidly plunge you into confusion and depression.

We have compiled this text with the aim of smoothing the transition from fledgling to competent doctor. It contains general information intended to reduce the feelings of terror which were so prominent during our first few months. As a result of the sheer complexity of the subject, a book such as this could never be completely comprehensive but we have included information which we hope will at least cushion the shock of commencing life as a junior doctor.

Acknowledgements

We are particularly grateful to Dr Alastair Forbes for his persistent attention to our project and for the endless contributions he provided: despite his more senior years he retains a humbling appreciation of the difficulties encountered by his juniors.

We would also like to thank Dr Mark Adams, Dr Stephen Beer, Dr Adrian Catterall, Dr John Chambers, Dr Martin Crook, Mrs Chrissie Green, Dr Derek Harrington, Dr Philip Mayne and Mrs Alison Missen for their constructive criticisms, and Mr Paul Dean for his essential help with the typescript.

Finally, and by no means least, we deeply appreciate what those around us have had to put up with throughout the preparation of this book and the simultaneous attention we had to give to the Part 1 MRCP exams.

Sample forms on pages 14, 15, 16, 17, 32, 33 and opposite page 30 are reproduced by permission of the Registrar General for England and Wales and the Controller of Her Majesty's Stationery Office.

Abbreviations Explained

AAFB	Alcohol and acid fast bacilli
ABG	Arterial blood gases
ACE inhibitors	Angiotensin converting enzyme inhibitors
ACTH	Adrenocorticotrophic hormone
ADH	Anti-diuretic hormone
AIDS	Acquired immune deficiency syndrome
ALP	Alkaline phosphatase
ALT	Alanine aminotransferase
ARC	AIDS-related complex
ARF	Acute renal failure
ASO titre	Anti-streptolysin-O titre
AST	Aspartate aminotransferase
ATN	Acute tubular necrosis
AXR	Abdominal X-ray
β-HCG	Beta-human chorionic gonadotrophin
bd	Twice daily
BP	Blood pressure
CCF	Congestive cardiac failure
CEA	Carcinoembryonic antigen
CFT	Complement fixation test
CK	Creatine kinase
CM	Cross match
CML	Chronic myeloid leukaemia
CMV	Cytomegalovirus
CNS	Central nervous system
COAD	Chronic obstructive airways disease
Conc	Concentration
CPK	Creatine phosphokinase
CPR	Cardiopulmonary resuscitation

CREST	Calcinosis, Raynaud's phenomenon, oesophageal dysfunction, sclerodactyly and telangiectasia
CRF	Chronic renal failure
CSF	Cerebrospinal fluid
CT	Computerised tomography
CVA	Cerebrovascular accident
CVP	Central venous pressure
CXR	Chest X-ray
DDAVP	Deamino-D-arginine vasopressin (desmopressin)
DHA	Dehydro-epiandrosterone
DI	Diabetes insipidus
DIC	Disseminated intravascular coagulation
DM	Diabetes mellitus
DVT	Deep vein thrombosis
ECG	Electrocardiogram
EDTA	Ethylene diamine tetra-acetic acid
ELISA	Enzyme linked immunosorbent assay
ENT	Ears, nose and throat
ERCP	Endoscopic retrograde cholangiopancreatography
ESR	Erythrocyte sedimentation rate
FBC	Full blood count
FDP	Fibrin degradation product
FEV	Forced expiratory volume
FFP	Fresh frozen plasma
FSH	Follicle stimulating hormone
FTA	Fluorescent treponemal antibody
FVC	Forced vital capacity
G-6-P	Glucose-6-phosphate
G & S	Group and Save
GH	Growth hormone
GIT	Gastrointestinal tract
GnRH	Gonadotrophin releasing hormone

γGT	Gammaglutamyl transpeptidase
GTN	Glyceryl trinitrate
H_2 blockers	Histamine type 2 receptor blockers
HBD	Hydroxybuterate dehydrogenase
HDL	High density lipoprotein
HDU	High dependency unit
HIAA	Hydroxyindole-acetic acid
HIV	Human immunodeficiency virus
HLA	Human leucocyte antigen
HMMA	4-hydroxy-3-methoxymandelic acid
HOCM	Hypertrophic obstructive cardiomyopathy
IBS	Irritable bowel syndrome
IBD	Inflammatory bowel disease
Ig	Immunoglobulin
IM	Intramuscular
INR	International Normalised Ratio
ISDN	Isosorbide dinitrate
ITU	Intensive treatment unit
IV	Intravenous
IVU	Intravenous urogram
JVP	Jugular venous pressure
KCl	Potassium chloride
LBBB	Left bundle branch block
LDH	Lactate dehydrogenase
LDL	Low density lipoprotein
LFT	Liver function tests
LH	Luteinising hormone
LMP	Last menstrual period
LVF	Left ventricular failure
Mane	Morning
MCH	Mean cell haemoglobin
MCHC	Mean cell haemoglobin concentration
MCV	Mean cell volume
MI	Myocardial infarction
MRI	Magnetic resonance imaging

MS	Multiple sclerosis
MST	Morphine sulphate tablets
MSU	Mid-stream sample of urine
NBM	Nil by mouth
Nocte	At night
NSAIDs	Non-steroidal anti-inflammatory drugs
od	Once daily
PA	Polyarteritis
PAN	Polyarteritis nodosa
PCV	Packed cell volume
PE	Pulmonary embolus
PEFR	Peak expiratory flow rate
PNH	Paroxysmal nocturnal haemoglobinuria
po	By mouth
PPD	Purified protein derivative
pr	per rectum
prn	When necessary
PSA	Prostate-specific antigen
PT	Prothrombin time
PTC	Percutaneous transhepatic cholangiography
PTH	Parathyroid hormone
PTT	Partial thromplastin time
qds	Four times per day
RA	Rheumatoid arthritis
RBC	Red blood cell
RTA	Renal tubular acidosis
rtPA	Recombinant tissue plasminogen activator
RVF	Right ventricular failure
SC	Subcutaneous
SL	Sublingual
SLE	Systemic lupus erythematosus
Stat	At once, immediately
tabs	Tablets
TB	Tuberculosis
TBG	Thyroxine binding globulin

tds	Three times per day
TENS	Transcutaneous electrical nerve stimulation
TG	Triglyceride
TIA	Transient ischaemic attack
TIBC	Total iron-binding capacity
TRH	Thyrotrophin releasing hormone
TSH	Thyroid stimulating hormone
U & E	Urea and electrolytes
UC	Ulcerative colitis
UTI	Urinary tract infection
V/Q scan	Ventilation-perfusion scan
VDRL	Venereal Disease Research Laboratory
VLDL	Very low density lipoprotein
VMA	Vanillymandelic acid
VT	Ventricular tachycardia
WCC	White cell count

1: General Information

General advice

Coping with stress

Those who deny that their year as a house person was difficult either had a lucky year or they are lying. From the moment you become a house officer you will be placed under varying levels of continual stress. Each person will cope with these stresses differently — if you feel you have reached boiling point, you should calmly walk away to somewhere more private and either: (a) scream; or (b) sob your heart out. Never be ashamed if you suddenly feel overwhelmed by your situation; most people feel like this at some stage. Talk to your peers or seniors — it's important to find someone to confide in.

Efficient use of time

There are those who work from 8.00 am to 7.00 pm every day but accomplish nothing. There are also those irritating individuals who work efficiently from 9.00 am to 11.00 am and finish everything. If you find yourself falling into the former category you need to look at your methods and try to improve your efficiency:

1 However busy you are, you should *never* miss your meals — patients can often wait and a break for food will dramatically improve your efficiency.

2 Before going home each night check that you have written all the necessary blood forms, X-ray forms etc. for the next day, and make a list of jobs to be done.

3 Always finish the job you are doing (unless an emergency arises) before going on to the next. This might sound obvious but it is difficult to concentrate on one job when being

continually disturbed by bleeps to write up laxatives, anti-emetics etc.

4 Encourage the ward staff to save up all your minor tasks for when you next visit the ward — but be sure to do them within a reasonable period of time or this system will fail.

5 To save time, irritation and embarrassment try to obtain all the laboratory results on your patients and ensure all of the necessary X-rays are available *before* the ward round. Also make sure that your patients know they are to be seen by their consultant — so that they don't disappear for a cigarette!

Writing in the notes

Initially it is difficult to know exactly what to write in the notes and how often. Medicolegally you are required to bring the notes up to date at least every third day. If the patient is acutely unwell or has been admitted recently ensure you make entries at least daily. The details you put down should allow a person not related to the case to understand the exact course of management even if they were to read the notes in 20 years' time.

Sum up how the patient feels (subjective details); details of examination (objective recordings); a general assessment of progress and an outline of your 'firm's' plans. It is useful to retain the acronym SOAP in your mind to give your entries meaning and fluidity:

*S*ubjective
*O*bjective
*A*ssessment   = SOAP
*P*lans

Write clearly and sign and date each entry. There is nothing more useless than writing something in the notes that somebody after you will be unable to read. If your signature is illegible then you should print your name and add your bleep number. Legible clear notes may sway the decision of a court in your favour in any ensuing legal proceedings!

General practitioners

It is easy to forget that most of the time your patients are looked after by their general practitioner (GP). You are a very important link between the two and everything you can do to smooth the transition from hospital care to community care will be much appreciated. If a patient with a particular problem is about to leave hospital phone his or her GP beforehand.

Other points

You are an important source of information for your patients and their relatives. Many patients are intimidated by ward rounds; if you have time, slip back and see them afterwards to check that they are happy.

Be sympathetic to requests from relatives to see you — this demand on your time may upset your plans but remember how much you would want to be kept fully informed if a close relative of yours were in hospital.

If you are being asked to talk to several members of the same family at many different times, it may be worth selecting a family representative with whom to communicate on a regular basis. Then suggest that other relatives keep up to date through this person.

Sister probably knows more than you about most things. If you forget this fact, she may let you know painfully; if you are lucky she will let you know subtly.

Bear in mind that you have to work as a team with the ward staff, nurse, phlebotomist etc. — it's important for both your patient's sake and your own sake to have a good working relationship; your life can be made very difficult otherwise.

Remember that you are not a registered practitioner and that responsibility lies with your senior house officer (SHO)/registrar. S/he will hopefully be willing to advise or help out when you are unsure. 'Good' house officers are those who contact their SHO/registrars when worried; 'bad' house officers are those who take on too much responsibility.

Make sure that colleagues don't dump everyday work onto you out of hours (such as re-writing drug charts or prescribing warfarin etc.) and beware of colleagues who may be less conscientious than yourself. If necessary re-check their management decisions — but be subtle about doing so.

Many colleagues fall out over the rota. You have to do each other favours but make sure that you balance out your work equally so that you have no lingering feelings of resentment.

Until junior doctor's hours are finally brought down to a reasonable level, house jobs will continue to be a severe hardship. Despite your seeming insignificance in making decisions on the management of your patients you nevertheless play a crucial part in the day-to-day running of your firm. Even when the pressure seems to be incredible, take comfort from this knowledge.

Bureaucracy

Financial matters

Doctors are, on the whole, notoriously poor at managing their financial affairs. We have included some basic points here to enlighten the generally uninitiated house officer about the confusions of his or her salary statement. Our knowledge has been improved by reading McKim Thompson, I. (1990) *Handbook for Hospital Junior Doctors*, British Medical Association, London, to which you are referred for further information if the following does not suffice.

Your pay slip

This seems to be a maze of random figures at first sight but with a little scrutiny it can be easily understood.

The basic salary for a house officer (1991–1992) is £12 100 p.a. Money may be *added* or *taken away* from this figure at source (i.e. before you can argue about it!).

ADDITIONS

1. Units of Medical Time (UMTs)

Doctors are paid on the basis of Units of Medical Time (UMTs):

1 UMT = 4 h

The basic salary payment accounts for the standard 40 h working week, i.e. 10 UMTs paid at Standard Rate.

There are 128 h remaining in the week (= 32 UMTs) which are worked 'on call' and are paid at Class 'A' UMT rate. This, would you believe, is worth 38% of the Standard Rate for a house officer.

The number of Class 'A' rate UMTs you receive will vary according to your rota:

'1 in 2' = 32/2 = 16 UMTs
'1 in 3' = 32/3 = 11 UMTs
'1 in 4' = 32/4 = 8 UMTs

Extra UMTs can be claimed in the following circumstances:
1 Internal cover for colleagues' duties.
2 Regular over-runs of shifts or early starts.
3 Teaching/research.
4 Administrative duties.

Sometimes you will feel put upon by your medical staffing department to do extra work with no clear information on how much you will receive for doing so. At such times you must be aware of your rights. For example, if you are asked to cover for a colleague who is away on sick or compassionate leave you can ask for an external locum to be found *or* claim Standard Rate UMTs if you work over and above your contracted hours.

You may find that you are contractually required to cover for a colleague who becomes suddenly unavailable for work (e.g. goes off sick) — if so ensure that you are paid Standard Rate UMTs if you have to work extra nights 'on call'.

2. London weighting

This can be claimed for living in London or its environs. The rates from 1st April 1991 are as follows:

London zone = £1292 p.a.
Fringe zone = £149 p.a.

There are also special arrangements for resident staff who receive free accommodation:

London zone = £359 p.a.
Fringe zone = £38 p.a.

If you are living in rented accommodation or you are paying a mortgage you are entitled to full London weighting; make sure Medical Staffing are aware of this. You may be asked to provide proof in the form of a rent book or mortgage certificate.

DEDUCTIONS

Deductions other than tax, pension and national insurance may *not* be made from your salary without your permission.

1. Income tax

This is a tax on income which is set at 25% for those earning under £1975/month (i.e. you!).

Taxable income = gross income − (superannuable pay + personal tax allowance) (see below)

Income tax is usually deducted at source in accordance with your Pay As You Earn (PAYE) code (tax code).

To calculate your PAYE code you need to add up your personal tax allowance. This is the money that can be earned without being taxed. It includes a sum set by the government (1991: £3295 for a single person) plus tax-free expenses, which for a newly qualified doctor are limited and include (according to the *Handbook for Hospital Junior Doctors*):

1 BMA subscription.
2 Medical defence subscription.
3 Damage to clothing.
4 Replacement of medical instruments.
5 General Medical Council (GMC) annual retention fee.
An example PAYE code calculation:

Tax allowance	£3290
Defence union subscription	£15
BMA subscription	£59
Total	£3364 = personal tax allowance

The last digit is ignored and a suffix letter, which denotes type of personal allowance (e.g. 'L' for a single person), is added. Thus the example PAYE code = 336L. The PAYE code can only be applied after first deducting contributions to the NHS superannuation scheme.

2. NHS superannuation scheme
This is an optional NHS scheme which provides a pension and a lump sum retirement allowance, payable on retirement at 60 years of age or over. The BMA has recommended that its members take up this option rather than choosing a personal scheme. The superannuable pay is 6% of your superannuable income; that is, 6% of your basic salary (excluding 'A' rate UMTs) will be subtracted at source into this pension fund.

3. National insurance contributions
This provides payments towards the cost of State redundancy and maternity entitlements as well as to the NHS. The contributions are earnings related and based on a percentage of the employee's total earnings. Contributions are also paid by your employers. For those earning £802–1690 per month these are:

Employee's rate = 2% on the first £226, and 9% thereafter
Employer's rate = 10.45%

Your contract

This legally binding document can normally be found amongst the wodge of papers thrust into your hands by Medical Staffing on your first day. Both you and an administrator of your employing authority should sign it *before* you start your job (in practice this often doesn't happen).

You MUST check that it outlines the following points:

1 Leave entitlement.

2 Annual salary including UMTs.

3 Date of start and end of employment.

4 Whether or not the job is a resident one.

5 The amount of notice of termination required to be given by you or your employer.

6 The limits of your contractual commitments (i.e. states those hours of duty you will be required to fulfil). Ensure this is the same as in your job description.

7 It should also contain a statement preventing your employers from making alterations (other than those required by law) to your salary without your prior permission.

Leave entitlement

Some health authorities will include weekends as days of holiday even though you would not necessarily be working them! You will however be allocated extra leave entitlement to account for this bizarre system. If non-worked weekends are included, your leave entitlement is 17.5 days per 6 months, whereas if non-worked weekends are not included you are only entitled to 13 days per 6 months.

Although you are not paid any extra for working public or NHS holidays, you are entitled to an extra day's holiday in lieu of these days if you work all of the day or up to 9.00 am on such a holiday. For example, if you work a weekend and the Monday is a bank holiday, stay until 9.00 am before handing over and going home and you will be due an extra day's holiday! However if you work the Sunday and Monday of a bank holiday weekend this will only give one extra day's holiday, not two.

N.B. 'Forewarned is forearmed': if you are working an internal cover system sort out your holidays very early on, otherwise you may find yourself short-changed at the end of your 6 months.

Sick leave

Those absent from duty owing to illness, injury or other disability receive the following sickness allowance:

Newly qualified house officers: 1 month's full pay and then nothing.

Those who have completed 4 months' employment: 1 month's full pay, 2 months' half pay, and then nothing.

Thus it is advisable to look into obtaining separate sickness insurance from an assurance company. Their representatives may well approach you with varying degrees of persuasion. If you find yourself being pestered unduly, contact the representative's head office and let them know that you are upset. This normally stops their advances quite quickly!

Defence union membership

As of 1st January 1990, the Government decided to indemnify NHS hospital doctors. This means that the Health Authority will accept financial liability for acts or omissions of doctors employed by them. This will not cover actions made outside those required by the Authority, e.g.:

1 Good Samaritan acts (e.g. helping the victim of a road traffic accident).

2 Private practice work including certificates (e.g. cremation forms).

Defence organisations will always support members in the above circumstances and will seek to clear the name of the doctor if at all possible — this is not the case for Crown

Indemnity under which circumstance a settlement could be agreed out of court to save money irrespective of the position of the doctor.

Useful addresses

Medical Defence Union, 3 Devonshire Place, London W1 2EA. Tel: 071–486 6181.

Medical Protection Society, 50 Hallam Street, London W1N 6DE. Tel: 071–637 0541.

Medical & Dental Defence Union of Scotland Ltd, 105 St Vincent Street, Glasgow G2 5EQ. Tel: 041–332 6646.

General Medical Council registration

It may seem a long way off when you start your first house job, but it is vital to ensure that you apply for *full* GMC membership in the last 2 weeks of your last house job. In theory you need to have your full GMC membership *before* starting an SHO post: some authorities would go as far as not letting you start the job if you fail to provide the necessary documentation.

To become fully registered you must first obtain a certificate of satisfactory service from your consultant at the end of *each* 6-month period of service, and send both of these to the dean of your medical school. If they are accepted then a Certificate of Experience will be issued with which you can apply to the GMC for full registration. If you have any problems, contact your medical school administration department.

The British Medical Association

If you are a member of the BMA you can contact your local office for advice on all sorts of matters (such as pay disputes, poor living conditions etc.). They will often take up the problem for you.

Ward paperwork

Consent forms

Most day-to-day ward procedures do not need formal *written consent*. However, this is required when the patient's ability to refuse treatment is removed (e.g. sedation for an endoscopy or a general anaesthetic), or when the procedure has well-known life-threatening complications (e.g. liver biopsy).

The consenting patient *must* understand what s/he is consenting to. In *all cases* you should take time to explain *simply* the exact nature of the procedure and why it is necessary. In a medicolegally ideal world you would also mention *all* the known complications and record your discussion in the notes. However, the already stressed patient may become overburdened by such anxieties. You must assess each situation separately and decide exactly how much to tell the patient. At the very least you should mention the most common complications and document the fact that you have done so in the notes. Consent forms are changing and some now specifically require you to document complications on the form. If you are in any doubt as to what these complications might be, ask the person who will perform the procedure.

For patients who are under 16 years of age, or demented, or unable for another reason to complete the form satisfactorily, a signature should be obtained from the next-of-kin or guardian.

NB: You may often find that you are being urged to complete the consent form as soon as possible. *Please* remember to take time over it since it may well save you from disaster in the future.

Accident forms

You will discover the delights of the Accident Form sooner rather than later. It is a form to prove that a qualified practitioner has seen and examined a patient who has had an accident whilst in hospital — commonly falling out of bed. The nursing staff are required to describe the sequence of events leading up to the accident.

You will be called at all times of the day and night and you will gradually learn when it is necessary to rush to the ward and assess the patient, and when formal assessment can be put off until later. When you do see the patient, ascertain that there has been no neurological or bony injury. In particular exclude a fractured neck of femur and loss of consciousness. Check for cuts, scratches and bruises. Any such injury should be clearly documented on the accident form and in the notes, with the use of diagrams as necessary. If there is no injury then there is probably no need to write in the notes. You should treat the report as a confidential statement and bear in mind that it may be used in evidence in any subsequent legal proceedings.

Sick notes
You may well be asked to fill in forms which enable patients to claim state benefit once they have left hospital (form **Med 3** — Fig. 1.1). You will have to write down the diagnosis and decide how long they should refrain from work. This can sometimes be very difficult. If you are uncertain ask your registrar or if in doubt give a shorter rather than longer time-spell. The patient must then go to his or her general practitioner (GP) for an extension as necessary.

If a patient needs to claim state benefit whilst in hospital, form **Med 10** can be signed by the nursing staff (Fig. 1.2).

TTAs (to take away) and controlled drug prescribing
In many hospitals the prescription sheet for drugs that patients are to take home incorporates a letter to the GP. A recent survey at Charing Cross Hospital, London, revealed that as many as 40% of these forms (also called TTHs/TTOs) were not

being suitably completed by house officers. Despite being an extremely tiresome task, TTAs are important from the patient's point of view. At the very least it is courteous to give the GP as much detail as possible:

1 Explain why the patient was admitted (i.e. diagnosis).
2 Describe the patient's treatment and subsequent progress.
3 Give details of follow-up.

Since discharge summaries take up to several weeks to reach the GP, your letter may help them manage their patients in the interim, should a problem arise.

IMPORTANT NOTES ON DRUG PRESCRIBING
1 Be cautious about sending patients home on benzodiazepines. They may have difficulty in sleeping for a few nights after discharge but this is preferable to them becoming dependent on these drugs.
2 Don't forget to prescribe from the PRN side of the inpatient chart (e.g. GTN, analgesia).
3 Always ensure that patients are suitably educated about the drugs that they are sent home on, e.g.: (a) what they are for; and (b) what interactions they must be careful of — if you don't tell them, nobody will. Take time to explain reducing courses carefully and give the patient written instruction about what to do.

Several pharmacies now offer a prescription counselling service whereby a pharmacist will sit down with a patient and discuss these various points with them at length.
4 Encourage your patients to keep a list of their medications on their person so that next time they attend a hospital, possibly in an emergency, the attending doctor will be able to make a rapid assessment of their tablets.

CONTROLLED DRUG PRESCRIBING
You must be sure to include the following information when prescribing controlled drugs for patients leaving hospital:

FOR SOCIAL SECURITY AND STATUTORY SICK PAY PURPOSES ONLY

NOTES TO PATIENT ABOUT USING THIS FORM

You can use this form either:

1. For Statutory Sick Pay (SSP) purposes – fill in Part A overleaf. Also fill in Part B if the doctor has given you a date to resume work. Give or send the completed form to your employer.

2. For Social Security purposes –
To continue a claim for State benefit fill in **Parts A** and C of the form overleaf. Also fill in Part B if the doctor has given you a date to resume work. **Sign and date the form** and give or send it to your local social security office QUICKLY to avoid losing benefit.

NOTE: To start your claim for State benefit you must use form SCI(Rev) if you are self-employed, unemployed or non-employed OR form SSPI(E) or SSPI(T) if you are an employee. For further details get leaflet NI16 (from DHSS local offices).

Doctor's Statement

In confidence to

Mr/Mrs/Miss/Ms ....

I examined you today/yesterday and advised you that

(a) You need not refrain from work

(b) you should refrain from work

for* ....

OR until† ....

Diagnosis of your disorder causing absence from work ....

Doctor's remarks

Doctor's signature

Date of signing

[illegible] ith & Hounslow F.P.C. 100977
[illegible]
Chiswick Health Centre.
Fishers Lane.
LONDON, W4.
[illegible]

Form Med 3
3/83

NOTE TO DOCTOR *†See inside front cover for notes on completion.*

Fig. 1.1 Sample form **Med 3**.

If you cannot fill this in yourself ask someone to do so and sign it for you.

A **TO BE COMPLETED IN ALL CASES** – PLEASE USE BLOCK LETTERS

Surname Mr/Mrs/Miss/Ms

First names

Present address

Postcode

	Date	Month	Year
Date of birth			

National Insurance Number

Works or Clock Number or Department

B. **If the doctor has given you a date to resume work**

Date you intend to start (or seek) work for any employer or as a self-employed person.

	Date	Month	Year
day			

For night shift workers only	Shift will begin at	Time	am/pm
	and end next day at	Time	am/pm

C. **FOR STATE BENEFIT CLAIMANTS ONLY**

Full name and address of employer (if employed)

| DECLARATION |

Remember: If you knowingly give wrong or incomplete information you may be prosecuted.

I declare that because of incapacity I have not worked since the date of my last claim.

I also declare that my circumstances and those of my dependants are and have been as last stated. (If there has been a change cross out this declaration and attach a signed and dated statement of new facts.)

The information given by me is true and complete.

I claim benefit.

I agree to my doctor giving medical information relevant to my claim to a doctor in the Regional Medical Service.

Sign here .... Date ....

If you have signed on behalf of the person claiming tick the box.

FOR SOCIAL SECURITY AND STATUTORY SICK PAY PURPOSES ONLY

NOTES TO PATIENT ABOUT USING THIS FORM

You can use this form either:

1. For Statutory Sick Pay purposes -

just fill in Part A overleaf and give or send the form to your employer or

2. For state benefit purposes -

To continue a claim for state benefit. Fill in Parts A and B of the form overleaf, sign and date it and send it to your local social security office QUICKLY to avoid losing benefit.

NOTE: To start your claim for State benefit you must use form SC1 (Rev) if you are self-employed, unemployed or non-employed OR form SSP1 (E) or SSP1 (T) if you are an employee. For further details get leaflet NI16 (from DHSS local offices).

NOTE TO HOSPITAL STAFF

For guidance on the completion of this form see notes on the back of the pad

---

HOSPITAL IN-PATIENT CERTIFICATE

To be filled in by an authorised person on the hospital staff

I certify that:-

1 Mr.
  Mrs.
  Miss
  Ms...

has received treatment as an

in-patient in this hospital continuously since and

D	M	Y

2 *(Complete (a) or (b) whichever applies)*

(a) is expected to remain an
    in-patient for at least a further

day
weeks

(b) was discharged from hospital on

D	M	Y

Is the patient a private patient? (YES or NO)

Signature
of certifier ....

Qualification or status ....

Date of Signing	D	M	Y

Hospital stamp

Form MED 10
3/83

Fig. 1.2 Sample form **Med 10**.

If you cannot fill this in yourself ask someone to do so and to sign it for you.

A. TO BE COMPLETED IN ALL CASES - PLEASE USE BLOCK LETTERS

Surname Mr/Mrs/Miss/Ms

First Names

Present Address
If claiming State benefit give address to which benefit is to be sent. If it is to be sent to some other person give his/her full name.

Postcode

	Date	Month	Year
Date of birth			

National Insurance Number

Works or clock number or department

B. FOR STATE BENEFIT CLAIMANTS ONLY

Full name and address of employer (if employed)

| Declaration |

Remember: If you knowingly give wrong or incomplete information you may be prosecuted.

I declare that because of incapacity I have not worked since the date of my last claim. I also declare that my circumstances and those of my dependants are and have been as last stated.

(If there has been a change cross out this declaration and attach a signed and dated statement of new facts).

The information given by me is true and complete.

I claim benefit.

Sign here .... Date ....

If you have signed on behalf of the person claiming tick this box:

If this certificate is given to you on discharge from a hospital, you will need a fresh sick note (Form MED 3) within a week from the doctor who is looking after you (your own doctor or the hospital doctor) UNLESS a sick note given to you before you went into hospital is still valid.

Printed in the UK for HMSO. D.8821870 67m 11/84.

1 Patient's name and address.
2 Date.
3 The name/form and strength of the preparation, e.g. MST Continus tablets 10 mg or pethidine tablets 50 mg. (You must put the form (e.g. tablets) *even if* this is implicit in the name of the drug or there is only one form of the drug.)
4 The number of dose units *or* the total quantity of the substance in figures *and* words, e.g. 56/fifty-six tablets, or 560/five hundred and sixty milligrams.
5 The dose to be taken: 'as directed' is the least that you can write.
6 All of the above needs to be in your own handwriting with your signature.

The final prescription should look like this:

1/6/92

Mrs A. D. Dict

The High Street

New Town

MST continus tablets 10 mg

20/twenty tablets

10 mg BD

A Bloggs

The following list shows those oral drugs which need to be prescribed under the regulations outlined above:

Amphetamine
Barbiturates
Buprenorphine
Cocaine
Diamorphine
Diethylpropion
Glutethimide
Mazindol
Meprobamate
Methylprylone
Morphine
Pentazocine
Pethidine
Phentermine
Quinalbarbitone

Notifiable diseases

Below is a list of those diseases which you are required by law to notify to your local medical officer for environmental health at the Department of Public Health. Decide in each case whether notification needs to be treated as urgent (i.e. by phone) or whether it could be dealt with by letter i.e. if the condition is highly infectious and potentially fatal, phone. Food poisoning can, on the other hand, usually be notified by letter.

There is always a doctor on call whom you can contact; the notification procedure varies in different areas but you may obtain the number from the microbiology laboratory. Alternatively (if you are ringing out of hours) try contacting the local town hall who should be able to put you in touch with the 'on call' doctor.

There is a very small fee payable for such notifications. Theoretically you could be fined for failing to notify.

Acute encephalitis
Acute poliomyelitis
Anthrax
Cholera
Diphtheria
Dysentery (amoebic/bacillary)
Food poisoning
Lassa fever
Leprosy
Leptospirosis
Malaria
Marburg fever
Measles
Meningitis
Meningococcal septicaemia
(without meningitis)
Mumps
Ophthalmia neonatorum

Paratyphoid fever
Plague
Rabies
Relapsing fever
Rubella
Scarlet fever
(Smallpox)
Tetanus

Tuberculosis
Typhoid fever
Typhus
Viral haemorrhagic fever
Viral hepatitis (all viral types)
Whooping cough
Yellow fever

NB: There are slight differences in Northern Ireland and Scotland.

In Northern Ireland the list includes
Gastro-enteritis (in those less than 2 years old)
Infective hepatitis

But the list excludes
Food poisoning
Infective jaundice
Leprosy
Malaria
Ophthalmia neonatorum
Tetanus

In Scotland the list includes
Continued fever
Erysipelas
Leptospiral jaundice
Membranous croup
Puerperal fever
Viral hepatitis

But the list excludes
Encephalitis
Infective jaundice
Tetanus
Tuberculosis

Requesting investigations

Request forms are tedious but it is important to remember that whoever interprets the results of these tests will be guided by the information you give them. It is often impossible to assess the significance of an X-ray, for example, without suitable clinical information. Give as much detail as possible about the case: help them to help you.

Problems with patients

Self-discharge and patients who refuse treatment

This situation always seems to arise when you least need it. If you are not tied up with some emergency you should:

1 Try to talk the patient out of his/her decision and explain why you feel it is necessary for him/her to stay.

2 Tell the patient clearly that s/he is leaving against medical advice.

Some patients will refuse treatment no matter what you say and it is a fundamental right of a conscious, mentally competent adult to do so. You should ask them to sign a self-discharge statement but you cannot compel him/her to do so.

If you are unsuccessful it is important to document the event in the case notes and if possible to obtain a staff nurse's signature as a witness to what has occurred. Very occasionally mental illness interferes with the patient's ability to make informed decisions. If you believe this to be the case, then you must seek the help of a psychiatrist who can decide whether it is appropriate to adopt legal powers of compulsory assessment and treatment under the regulations of the Mental Health Act 1983.

Mental Health Act 1983

We have included here an outline of the Act as it is likely to affect you.

SECTION 4 – EMERGENCY ADMISSION (72 h)
Applied for by the nearest relative *or* social worker *and* any doctor who has seen the patient in the past 24 h.

Grounds

1 Urgent necessity.
2 Mental disorder requiring hospital admission.
3 Danger to himself/herself or others.

Treatment of urgent necessity may be given under common law. This section is useful for patients in Casualty who have taken a life-threatening overdose but are trying to leave.

SECTION 5(2) — POWERS OF INPATIENT RESTRAINT
Application as for Section 4. Grounds as for Section 4 except that the patient is already in hospital.

NB: The powers of compulsory treatment of mental disorder *do not* give you the automatic right to treat any concurrent physical illness. This aspect of compulsory restraint is frequently misunderstood.

It is accepted however that the doctor in charge of the patient *does* have the right to give immediate treatment in life-threatening situations without the patient's consent.

Jehovah's Witnesses

A member of this religious sect may well refuse a blood transfusion on religious grounds. If, after explanation of the potential risks involved, they still refuse then they should sign an appropriate statement. You must then abide by this wish.

Christian Scientists

This particular group believe in spiritual or divine healing and often refuse conventional medical treatment. Again, after discussion, they should sign the appropriate form and you should respect their wishes.

Human immunodeficiency virus testing

Most hospitals now have specific policies for dealing with this delicate topic. These should be readily available for reading on all wards. The most important considerations are: the need to obtain consent (written if possible); and for the patient to undergo counselling.

Counselling

The patient should receive sufficient information about the procedure to allow him/her to make a balanced decision on whether or not to be tested. Inform patients why you feel the test is necessary but remember that they may know very little about HIV or AIDS. You must therefore:

1 Explain that HIV is the virus that causes AIDS.

2 Explain that being HIV positive is not synonymous with having AIDS or ARC.

3 Explain that on current evidence asymptomatic individuals have a 50% chance of developing AIDS after 10 years of HIV infection — thus it is not an immediate death sentence. Obviously if you are proposing a test to patients with suggestive symptoms or signs this percentage is increased.

4 Explain that there are support groups and trusts available for advice 24 hours/day if the patient were to be found to be HIV positive.

5 Explain the benefits of knowing their HIV status: (a) if found to be HIV positive then their immune status (T-cell count) can be monitored regularly and should it fall below a critical level then treatment can be instigated, thus delaying the onset of AIDS or ARC; (b) by being aware of their condition they would hopefully present earlier with opportunistic infections etc., thus making treatment easier; and (c) they would be able to reduce the spread by engaging in 'safer sex'.

6 You must point out potential disadvantages of having an HIV test such as the possible need to declare that they have had a test on life assurance forms. They may subsequently be refused a life insurance policy even if HIV negative.

If you have covered the above details then ask the patient whether s/he would be prepared to have a positive test. If not, arrange for further counselling. It should be possible to contact a suitable person via your social work department.

If a patient refuses a test s/he must be treated as HIV positive.

NB: Standard tests detect antibody to infecting virus which commonly appears a few weeks after infection but in an unknown proportion of patients, this takes many months or even years.

Death of a patient

Although you may become very used to dealing with death, never take the subject lightly. Your lack of thought or thoroughness can cause the patient's relatives much distress. You need to:
1 Confirm death.
2 Talk to relatives should they wish it.
3 Complete the death certificate.
4 Complete the cremation form as necessary.
5 Contact the patient's GP.

Only 1 and 2 need to be done immediately if the patient dies at night.

Confirming death

This aspect of your job appears to be omitted from many medical school curricula despite it being an integral part of your work. If you're lucky the procedure can be carried out by nursing staff in some hospitals — particularly useful at night! However this policy is not officially condoned by the nurse's governing body, the United Kingdom Central Council (UKCC).

If you are busy, always deal with sick patients before going to the ward to confirm a death but remember that the nursing staff cannot prepare the body until certified dead by you. You should confirm that:

1 The pupils are fixed and (usually) dilated.
2 There are no palpable carotid pulsations.
3 There are no heart or breath sounds heard over 1 min.
4 The patient is unresponsive to painful stimuli (e.g. pressing firmly on the sternum).

Write the above details in the notes and give the time and date of death, signing your name clearly.

Talking to relatives

This is an important part of your job and although the situation may be difficult for all involved, you must never avoid relatives. Hopefully you will have spoken to many of them previously and all you need to do is to offer your condolences. Most relatives are very grateful for what you, and the nursing staff, did for their late relative.

Postmortems

Sometimes your team may request a postmortem in the interests of scientific curiosity. Written consent from the next-of-kin or executor of the will is required. It may be very difficult to ask the relatives to give permission for postmortems but they are often important to clarify the cause of death. Your registrar should have faced this situation many times — watch him/her at work to get an idea of the way to approach the task. The body legally belongs to the next-of-kin and even if the deceased has given written instructions that an autopsy should be performed, without the permission of the next-of-kin or executor, you cannot do one.

HINTS FOR SUCCESS
1 Stress the fact that it is in the interests of the family and their

descendants to know the exact cause of death.

2 Point out that postmortems are quite usual, that the body will not be disfigured and that the face will not be touched.

3 Dispel any misconception they may have, that the body will be used for experiments or for teaching anatomy.

You must never use the threat of the case being referred to the Coroner should they not let you perform one.

NB: Relatives will probably want to know the findings. Take care not to forget this request.

Death certificates

1 It is often more difficult than you may think to decide exactly what was the cause of death. The death certificate should be completed with a *cause* of death and not a *mode* of death. Because in the past confusion has arisen over this important distinction, the Office of Population Census and Surveys supplied a comprehensive list of Modes of Death (Table 1.1). Should you fail to make this distinction then the Registrar of Deaths *may* refer the case to the Coroner.

2 Put what the patient died *from* and not what they died *with*. For example, if the patient died from a myocardial infarction and you mention that they had a bed sore, the Coroner might request an inquest.

If you are uncertain about the cause of death discuss the problem with a more senior colleague. You could consult the *International Statistical Classification of Diseases, Injuries and Causes of Death*, which should be available in your hospital. Alternatively contact the Registrar of Deaths (who may well have an office in your hospital). If your completion of the death certificate is unsatisfactory (i.e. rejected by the Registrar) then this will cause delay to mourning relatives.

WHO CAN SIGN THE DEATH CERTIFICATE?

The doctor who signs the certificate must be the one who

Table 1.1 Modes of death (terms unsuitable for giving as a cause of death)

Asphyxia
Asthenia
Brain failure
Cachexia
Cardiac failure (not further qualified)
Coma
Debility (general)
Exhaustion
Heart failure (not further qualified)
Hepatic failure
Hepatorenal failure
Kidney failure
Liver failure
Liver and kidney failure
Renal failure
Respiratory arrest
Shock
Syncope
Uraemia
Vagal inhibition
Vasovagal attack

attended the deceased in his/her last illness. If that doctor has gone away and there is no one else who can sign, then the Coroner will have to be informed. 'Attendance' is not defined but is usually taken to mean seeing the patient on at least two occasions. If you see a patient moribund in Casualty who dies within a few hours, this will not therefore entitle you to sign the certificate. You must also have seen the patient within a reasonable period before death (i.e. within 14 days). In the case of a cremation certificate (see below) you MUST have seen the patient *both* within 14 days *and after* death.

There is a question on the certificate which asks whether the patient was 'seen/not seen after death by me'. This is only included to help the Registrar to decide whether or not to report the death to the Coroner.

If you (or another hospital doctor) are unable to complete the certificate because the above criteria are not fulfilled, the

deceased's GP may be willing to sign the certificate if the
patient has died from the culmination of a known chronic
illness. If not, you will have to refer the death to the Coroner.
Should you refer the case to the Coroner then there is no
need for you to complete the death certificate — in all other
circumstances you have a statutory right to sign the certificate.

Concerning the Coroner

Contrary to popular belief, there is *no* statutory duty laid upon
a doctor to report a death to the Coroner. This is the duty of
the Registrar of Deaths (or in Scotland, the Procurator Fiscal).
However a system of cordial co-operation exists whereby
'coroner's cases' are reported directly to the Coroner by the
doctor. There are endless lists of examples of suitable referral
cases but these lists never seem to cover the cases you are
dealing with — therefore we have not included a list here. If
you do refer the case to the Coroner you should officially initial
the death certificate at 'A' on the reverse. In practice the
Coroner will complete the certificate and you do not normally
need to bother filling one in.

   If you are in any doubt about whether a certain case should
be referred to the Coroner, consult your superiors or ask to
speak to the Coroner's Officer (who is a police officer). In many
instances the style of your approach can greatly influence the
reply you get. For example, if you are dealing with a case in
which the patient died with a tracheostomy *in situ* you may
want to check with the Coroner's Officer whether or not this
comes under the heading of a patient dying before complete
recovery from an operation. Since your approach in these
matters can greatly influence the outcome, it is important to
think carefully before proceeding.

NB: If you do discuss the case informally with the Coroner or
his or her Officer *do not* initial the certificate at 'A' on the

reverse because you will produce the exact delay you had sought to avoid.

Once completed, it is, strictly speaking, the doctor's duty to deliver the certificate to the Registrar but in practice it is usually the relatives who do so. Certification may await postmortem results but if the relatives want a certificate for funeral purposes you should issue one and initial it at 'B' on the reverse (Fig. 1.3).

Death of a war pensioner

If a deceased person had a war pension, this may be transferable to his widow, particularly if the death certificate is suitably worded to demonstrate a direct connection between the pensioned disability and the cause or hastening of death. There is *no* statutory duty to report such cases to the Coroner. It is the Secretary of State who ultimately decides whether transfer is suitable but you can greatly aid the widow's claim by what you put as the cause of death.

Cremation forms

If a patient is to be cremated (the majority are) you will be required to complete form B, the Certificate of Medical Attendance, of the cremation form. Remember that for cremation forms you need to have 'attended' the patient within 14 days *and* you *must* see the patient after death. If the deceased is to undergo a postmortem, wait for the results before completing form B.

Cremations do not need to be notified to the Coroner unless the death fulfills the criteria in the previous section.

It is important to note that the fee you receive for completing these forms (popularly known as 'ash cash') is taxable. Thus you should keep a record of this income.

We have included a sample cremation form completed with standard data (Fig. 1.4). Make sure that the cause of death on form B is *identical* to that given on the death certificate, otherwise you will cause delays.

Spreading the news

You should make a point of informing the following people of
the death of a patient:

1 The consultant — easy to forget because s/he may not visit
the ward every day. Inform him/her as soon as possible of any
unexpected deaths.

2 The relevant team the next morning if the death occurred at
night.

3 The patient's GP. *Don't forget this* because they may not
receive a summary for several weeks and there is nothing more
embarrassing than meeting the relatives of a deceased person if
you are not aware that the relative has died.

Miscellaneous

Disclosure of information

In a 1989 booklet, the GMC states that a doctor has a clear
duty 'strictly to observe the rule of professional secrecy by
refraining from disclosing voluntarily to ANY THIRD PARTY
information about a patient which he has learnt directly as a
result of his professional capacity as a registered medical
practitioner' *Professional Conduct and Discipline: Fitness to
Practise*, General Medical Council. Thus, no employer, member of a patient's family (including spouse), solicitor, clergy-
man, or other person acting on the patient's behalf or member
of the media should be given *any* confidential information
without the patient's written consent.

In cases of accidents which draw press enquiries, be careful
not to mention the patient's name until you know the relatives
have been informed. In most cases it is wise to refer press
enquiries to the designated person within the hospital.

Police enquiries

You may feel it is somehow your duty to disclose all you know about a patient to the police; for example you may suspect, or in fact have been told by the patient, that he was involved in a crime. However, it is important to note that the GMC guidelines mentioned above refer to *any* third party and this includes the police. In cases of serious crime you have a citizen's duty to the community to report a crime to the police. Even information obtained solely through your doctor–patient relationship may be disclosed if you feel that failure to do so might bring harm to an innocent third party or cause risk to the community. This citizen's duty may outweigh your ethical constraints of confidentiality.

If, in less serious cases, you feel strongly that you must keep your knowledge confidential you will be in no legal danger provided you do not take active steps to assist a criminal to avoid detection or to escape.

If you are specifically requested by the police to forward information about a patient in the form of a statement, you need not fear prosecution as long as you present the truth: *but* you may be ethically wrong in doing so and on this conflict between law and ethics you must make your own decision. In these difficult circumstances try to obtain the permission of the patient concerned to disclose the information. If in doubt contact your Defence organisation for advice on how to proceed safely.

Fitness to drive

Patients will frequently ask you about their ability to drive after various illnesses. You are able to advise them but it is not *your* responsibility but *your patient's* to notify the DVLC about their current physical condition. Each case will be assessed by the DVLC separately.

The regulations are different for those holding an ordinary licence and those holding or wishing to hold an HGV or PSV licence.

FREDK. W. PAINE
BRYSON HOUSE, HORACE ROAD
KINGSTON UPON THAMES, SURREY KT1 2SL
Telephone: 01-546 7472

CREMATION ACTS, 1902 and 1952

Statutory Rules and Orders, 1930, 1952 and 1965

These Forms are Statutory. All the questions must be answered, therefore, to make the Certificate effective for the purposes of Cremation.

These medical certificates are regarded as strictly confidential. The right to inspect them is confined to the Secretary of State, the Ministry of Health, and the Chief Officer of a Police Force.

FORM B

(1) This form is not to be used in the case of a Coroner's Inquest.

CERTIFICATE OF MEDICAL ATTENDANT

I am informed that application is about to be made for the cremation of the remains of:—

(*Name of Deceased*) ....

(*Address*) ....

(*Occupation or Description*) .... (*Age*) ....

(2) All the questions must be answered. Lines or Dashes are insufficient.

Having attended the Deceased before death, and seen and identified the body after death, I give the following answers to the questions set out below:—

1.	On what date, and at what hour, did he or she die?	.92
2.	What was the place where the deceased died? (Give address and say whether own residence, lodgings, hotel, hospital, nursing home, etc.)	WARD M3 St Elsewhere.
3.	Are you a relative of the deceased? If so, state the relationship.	NO
4.	Have you, so far as you are aware, any pecuniary interest in the death of the deceased?	NO
5.	(a) Were you the ordinary medical attendant of the deceased? (b) If so, for how long?	(a) NO (b) —
6.	(a) Did you attend the deceased during his or her last illness? (b) If so, for how long?	(a) YES (b) THREE DAYS
7.	When did you last see the deceased alive? (Say how many days or hours before death.)	TWO HOURS
8.	(a) How soon after death did you see the body? (b) What examination of it did you make?	(*The doctor must see the body after death*) (a) 72 HOURS (AFTER WEEKEND) (b) EXTERNAL
8A.	If the deceased died in a hospital* at which he was an in-patient, has a post-mortem examination been made by a registered medical practitioner of not less than five years' standing who is neither a relative of the deceased nor a relative or partner of yours and are the results of that examination known to you?	NO
9.	What was the cause of death? I. Immediate cause Morbid conditions, if any, giving rise to immediate cause (state in order proceeding backwards from immediate cause). II. Other morbid conditions (if important) contributing to death but not related to immediate cause.	(a) BRONCHOPNEUMONIA due to (b) .... due to (c) CARCINOMA OF BRONCHUS. EMPHYSEMA, DIABETES MELLITUS (OVER)

(3) If the death has been reported to Coroner for any reason, this should be stated in answer to question 18.

Fig. 1.4 Sample cremation form B.

10. (a) What was the mode of death?
(Say whether syncope, coma, exhaustion, convulsions, etc.) (a) COMA

(b) What was its duration in days, hours, or minutes? (b) TWELVE HOURS

11. State how far the answers to the last **two** questions are the result of your own observations, or are based on statements made by others. If on statements made by others, say by whom.
MY OWN
OR STAFF OF M3.

12. (a) Did the deceased undergo any operation during the final illness or within a year before death? (a) NO

(b) If so, what was its nature and who performed it? (b)

13. By whom was the deceased nursed during his or her last illness?
(Give names, and say, whether professional nurse, relative, etc. If the illness was a long one, this question should be answered with reference to the period of four weeks before the death.)
STAFF OF M3.

14. Who were the persons (if any) present at the moment of death?
FAMILY AND STAFF OF M3

15. In view of the knowledge of the deceased's habits and constitution, do you feel any doubt whatever as to the character of the disease or the cause of death?
NO

16. Have you any reason to suspect that the death of the deceased was due, directly or indirectly, to

(a) Violence ....

(b) Poison .... NO

(c) Privation or neglect? ....

(4) When the certificate for registration has been given by authority of the Coroner, this fact should be stated.

17. Have you any reason whatever to suppose a further examination of the body to be desirable? NO

18. Have you given the certificate required for registration of death? If not, who has? YES .

Important
Please
complete
this section

IMPORTANT
Pacemakers can cause an explosion if left in a body which is cremated. Radio-active implants are a health hazard.
Please answer the following questions by ticking the appropriate boxes.   YES NO
   i) Has the deceased been fitted with (a) a cardiac pacemaker?
                       (b) a radio-active or other implant?
   ii) If the answer to (a) or (b) above is in the affirmative: Has this been removed?
   NOTE: CREMATION MAY BE REFUSED IF A PACEMAKER IS NOT REMOVED

I Hereby Certify that the answers given above are true and accurate to the best of my knowledge and belief, and that I know of no reasonable cause to suspect that the deceased died either a violent or an unnatural death or a sudden death of which the cause is unknown or died in such place or circumstances as to require an inquest in pursuance of any Act.

NAME IN
BLOCK CAPITALS .... (*Signature*) ....

(*Address*) : ....

....

(*Date*) .... (*Telephone*) .... (*Registered Qualifications*) ....

NOTE – This certificate must be handed or sent in a closed envelope by the medical practitioner who signs it, to the medical practitioner who is to give the confirmatory certificate in Form C except in a case where question 8A above is answered in the affirmative, in which case, the certificate must be so handed or sent to the Medical Referee.

The bearer of the certificate can act as the agent of the medical attendant, and to him may be handed the closed envelope for delivery to the other medical practitioner.

* The term 'hospital' as used here means any institution for the reception and treatment of persons suffering from illness or mental disorder, any maternity home, and any institution for the reception and treatment of persons during convalescence.

In Table 1.2 we list those illnesses you will be presented with regularly on a general medical or surgical ward. For further information please refer to *Medical Aspects of Fitness to Drive* (1988), published by the Medical Commission on Accident Prevention. This is an extensive text and is worth obtaining to read about the areas we have not covered.

Table 1.2   Medical aspects of fitness to drive

Disease or symptoms	Advice to holder of an ordinary licence	Advice to holder of an HGV or PSV licence
(a) Neurological system		
Epilepsy	Barred from driving if recent fits have occurred. Licence can be applied for if patient remains fit-free for 2 years or has fits only whilst asleep for a period of 3 years. This will be a limited duration licence. Avoid driving for 6 months during treatment changes	A person may not hold a vocational licence if they have had a fit after the age of 5 years. In doubtful cases arbitration will be required
Single fit	Barred from driving initially. If no cause is found DVLC must still be informed — they will probably invoke a 1 year ban	As for epilepsy
Vertigo and TIAs	Notify DVLC. 3 months symptom-free period required	Permanent ban
Any cause of muscle weakness, post-CVA, sensory defects, MS	Depends on severity. Assess each case separately, and ask for advice	If symptoms are persistent or recurrent, driving banned

Table 1.2 (*continued*)

Disease or symptoms	Advice to holder of an ordinary licence	Advice to holder of an HGV or PSV licence
(b) Cardiovascular system disorders		
Myocardial infarction	Notify DVLC. Avoid driving within 2 months	Tough restrictions. Banned if: **1** ECG shows typical Q waves, ST and T wave changes, LBBB, or complete heart block **2** If it is the second myocardial infarction (or the first but the patient has associated peripheral vascular disease) **3** If a coronary angiogram shows significant occlusion or an exercise stress test shows significant ST depression. **4** If any of the complications listed below applies
Angina	Avoid driving if angina is easily provoked by it	No significant angina is allowed
Complete heart block	Driving is forbidden. Notify the DVLC. Driving is allowed from 1 month after insertion of a pacemaker as long as its function is regularly checked	Pacemaker or not, driving is permanently forbidden
Postural hypotension, impaired concentration, syncopal attacks, transient faintness	Avoid driving until problem solved	Ectopics disappearing with exercise are allowed. Other arrhythmias, vasovagal or syncopal attacks result in a ban
Aortic aneurysm	No restrictions	Banned
Anticoagulant therapy	No restrictions	Banned

Table 1.2   *(continued)*

Disease or symptoms	Advice to holder of an ordinary licence	Advice to holder of an HGV or PSV licence
(c) Endocrine/metabolic system		
Diabetes	Notify the DVLC. A limited (1, 2 or 3-year licence) will normally be issued, depending on quality of control, complications and follow up. Insulin-dependent diabetics in particular should show: **1** A reasonable understanding of their disease **2** A reasonable control of their blood sugar **3** No frequent, sudden or unexplained hypoglycaemic attacks	The patient should notify the DVLC if control worsens or they switch to insulin. Cases need individual review. New applicants for these licences must not be insulin-dependent.

Adapted from *Medical Aspects of Fitness to Drive*, after Palmer, K. T. (1988) *Notes for the MRCGP*, Blackwell Scientific Publications, Oxford.

OTHER CONSIDERATIONS

1 The locomotor system: restriction is largely a matter of common sense. Officially most conditions resulting in impaired mobility of one or more limbs should be referred to the DVLC. Adaptations may be required to various classes of vehicle. The restrictions for holders of a vocational licence are similar but obviously stricter.

2 Anaesthetics: patients should not drive for 24–48 h after a general anaesthetic. Make sure you point this out to patients attending the Day Surgical Unit.

The rehabilitation team

There is a multidisciplinary team of individuals whose aim it is to rehabilitate patients back to as normal a life as possible following various debilitating illnesses, commonly strokes.

Their role is often under-rated and it is easy to miss their importance, particularly in helping your patients who will need support on returning home.

The team typically consists of:

1 The physiotherapist, who is concerned with mobility, balance and the prevention of contractures.

2 The occupational therapist, who is able to assist the patient to regain the ability to perform various tasks of daily living and to assess the patient's home in an endeavour to make it easily habitable on return.

3 The social worker, who is responsible for social support including the arrangements for 'meals on wheels', home help etc. and for arranging future placement if a return home is not possible.

4 The speech therapist, who can help to improve problems with dysphasia and/or dysarthria or dysphagia.

5 The nursing staff, who are vitally important in maintaining patient continence, preventing the development of pressure sores, health education, dealing with relatives etc.

6 The community nurses can be alerted to patients who are going home and may need various health indices checked, e.g. BP, BM Stix, before returning to clinic.

TYPES OF RESIDENCE AVAILABLE FOR THE ELDERLY

Depending on the patient's ability to look after himself, and the degree of family support, a decision will need to be made about placement after discharge from hospital. If going home is out of the question, then there are other options:

1 Sheltered accommodation: this consists of units that are supervised by a warden; their only duty is confined to daily checks to see that all is well with their residents. Most wardens, however, are very involved with their residents and can be very helpful in sorting out any problems you may have with your elderly patients. Residents must be reasonably self-sufficient.

2 Part III accommodation (old people's homes, residential homes). Patients considered for this option need to have a minimal degree of competence in the activities of daily living, e.g.:
- able to get in and out of a bed unaided
- able to eat and dress without help
- mobile enough to get to the bathroom
- fully continent.

3 Patients who do not fulfil the criteria for either of the above may be settled in either:
- long-stay geriatric wards — accessed by referral to your hospital geriatric team
- nursing homes — private or council run. There may be somebody in your hospital responsible for placing the elderly into nursing homes (e.g. the Homefinder Team).

There are often waiting lists of various lengths for the above options and it is worth considering placement the day your patient is admitted.

The mini-mental test score
It is very useful to have a simple method of assessing the mental function of your elderly patients — particularly in Casualty. There are various mental test scores available; some longer, some shorter. Which one you use doesn't really matter so long as you are consistent, and hopefully those in your team use the same one. Below is an example of a quick assessment but check with your registrar to see if s/he has any preferences.

The patient scores one point for each *complete* correct answer to the following questions, to a maximum of 10.
1 Name.
2 Date of birth.
3 Day, month, year.
4 Place where patient is at the time of assessment.
5 Recognising two people (e.g. yourself and a nurse).

6 Recall an address, e.g. 10 Oak Lane, New Town, England.
7 Dates of World War I (1914–1918).
8 Name of the Monarch.
9 Name of the Prime Minister.
10 Count down from 1 to 20 without a mistake.
Document your results in the notes.

Terminal care

There comes a stage when the treatment of a patient changes
from possible cure to symptom control. When considering the
management of the terminally ill you should think about the
effects of the disease in three areas: physical; social; and
psychological.

PHYSICAL

Pain
See under Analgesia (Chapter 2). No patient should ever be in
pain; give as much as necessary to prevent distress.

Anorexia and nausea
1 Small doses of steroids (e.g. 5 mg prednisolone od) may help
to improve their appetite.
2 Nausea and vomiting may be alleviated by the regular
prescription of anti-emetics.

Metastases
Steroids may reduce the neurological complications of cord
compression or cerebral oedema, with a limited but often very
worthwhile improvement. The initial management is: oral or
IV dexamethasone 8 g/day in divided doses.

Dyspnoea
Diazepam may be useful in controlling the distressed patient.

SOCIAL

Respect any wish the patient or family may have for the patient to be allowed to die at home. Make sure they receive adequate support either from friends, relatives or from social services (or both). Involve the patient's GP and the Macmillan team of nurses to ensure that the patient dies in comfort at home.

PSYCHOLOGICAL

No matter how busy you are, you should always take time to explain to both the patient and relatives the nature and prognosis of the patient's disease. Do not be frightened about being frank but always show compassion. Both you and the nursing staff play an important role in seeing the patient and family through their ordeal.

We realise the above is an almost flippant reference to this crucially important subject. If you have the chance, attend a course on the management of the terminally ill patient; failing that, obtain a book on the subject. Discuss the subject of pain control further with your specialists.

Preparing patients for investigations

If one of your patients is to undergo a procedure that you know little about, explain your ignorance to the patient and go with them to see what is involved. You will then be able to explain to other patients in the future exactly what they will go through.

For each investigation, make a list of:

1 Whether consent is necessary.
2 What preparations are required — e.g. blood tests, NBM etc.
3 Post-procedure details – e.g. how long the patient needs to be rested for, when they can eat etc.
4 Potential post-procedure side-effects.

Table 1.3 lists some information on the most common investigations.

Table 1.3 Common investigations

Test	Consent	NBM	Fluids only	Bowel preparation	Comments
(a) Gastrointestinal tract					
Barium meal/ swallow	No	Yes	—	No	Patient can eat as soon as they return to the ward
Barium enema	No	No	Yes	Yes	Check what preparation your X-ray department expects
Barium follow through	No	Yes	No	No/yes	Low-residue diet for the previous 2–3 days. Advise patient that procedure may take many hours and may involve them being positioned in various and sometimes unusual positions
Gastroscopy	Yes	Yes	No	No	Patients are normally given a sedative on reaching the endoscopy suite. They can eat once their gag reflex returns. Watch out for signs of perforation, particularly if undergoing oesophageal dilatation: dysphagia, neck pain, fever, bleeding, surgical emphysema
ERCP	Yes	Yes	No	No	Need FBC, clotting studies and G & S, IV access and antibiotics, pre- and post-operatively (check what is preferred). May be given a sedative in the endoscopy suite. If there are no complications, drink at 2–4 h: full diet next day. Watch out for signs of perforation: dysphagia, neck pain, fever, bleeding. Also watch out for pancreatitis and cholangitis

Table 1.3 (*continued*)

Test	Consent	NBM	Fluids only	Bowel preparation	Comments
Colonoscopy	Yes	No	Yes	Yes	Check what preparation your endoscopist expects. Many preparation protocols can cause moderate dehydration and diarrhoea. Give patient full instructions on what to expect
Sigmoidoscopy Rigid	No	No	No	No	Generally a minor procedure carried out on the ward or in outpatients
Flexible	Yes	No	Yes	Yes	Similar to colonoscopy
(b) *Others* Angiography	Yes	Yes	—	No	Check clotting, FBC and U & E: need G & S. Bed rest for 12 h afterwards (but depends on unit)
Bronchoscopy	Yes	Yes	No	—	Require premedication to reduce secretions and to sedate the patient — check with operator. Check clotting and FBC. Some operators require formal respiratory function tests and ABGs. Watch for cyanosis, hypotension, tachycardia, dysrhythmia, haemoptysis, dyspnoea and bronchospasm
Bone scan	No	No	—	No	Patient will receive an injection. Warn them that the whole procedure may take several hours
CT	No	+/−	—	No	A non-invasive procedure but warn the patient of the claustrophobic environment and the possibility that they will be injected with contrast medium. Need to be NBM for some GIT scans

Table 1.3 *(continued)*

Test	Consent	NBM	Fluids only	Bowel preparation	Comments
Echocardiography	No	No	—	—	Non-invasive
IVU	No	Yes	—	—	They will receive an injection
MRI	No	+ / –	—	—	NBM if investigating bowel. Warn patient of the extremely claustrophobic environment and the loud noise
Myelography	Yes	No	—	—	May receive a light sedative. Maintain on bed rest for 6 h afterwards. Drink plenty of fluids. May develop a headache — see under Lumbar puncture in Chapter 3
PTC	Yes	Yes	No	No	Warn them of the need to co-ordinate the holding of breath
V/Q scan	No	No	—	—	Warn patient they will inspire xenon and be injected

NB: Warn any patient receiving contrast medium that they may experience a 'warm-flush' after the contrast is given.

Ultrasonography (No consent required. Painless)

Kidney	No preparation
Gall bladder	Fasting 6 h: can drink water *only*
Liver	Fasting 6 h: can drink water *only*
Pancreas	Fasting 6 h: can drink water *only*
Spleen	Fasting 6 h: can drink water *only*
Aorta	Fasting 6 h: can drink water *only*
Lymph nodes	Fasting 6 h: can drink water *only*
Pelvis	Eat and drink. Full bladder required: patient must empty their bladder 2.5 h beforehand and then drink plenty
Thyroid	Nil preparation
Carotids	Nil preparation

The night round checklist

It is surprising how many house officers fail to go round the wards last thing at night and wonder why they are disturbed at 2.00 am for a simple task. You should try to go around all of the wards with patients you are covering before you go to bed. If they are scattered all over the hospital it is sometimes easier to ring round the relevant wards. Make sure that your round is after the night drug-round since this is when most problems come to light. Your main aims are to:

1 Attend to any patients that the nursing staff are worried about.

2 Check that there are no 'dodgy' venflons.

3 Check that patients receiving IV fluids have enough written up to last them through to the morning and check that various drug infusions will last the night. If they look as if they might run out enquire whether the night sister will make the next lot when necessary. If not, you could make up a supply to be left in the fridge ready for use (e.g. heparin, insulin infusions).

4 Check that patients are written-up for night sedation – see under Night sedation (Chapter 2)

If you are contacted at night to attend to a simple task having already done your night round:

1 Check that the patient is 'yours'.

2 Ask the night sister if she would mind helping.

3 Find out why you weren't asked to do it before!

2: Pharmaceutical Practical Advice

To pass the pharmacology section of your final exams you have to have a good knowledge of drug uses, how they work and what side-effects you may encounter. You will rarely, if ever, be asked to show that you know how to give the drug. Unfortunately, from day one of your job, you will be giving many of the drugs you have learnt about, and often, to acutely sick patients who need them urgently; and you may find yourself deficient in the practical knowledge of how to give them. This section aims to fill the gap between academic and practical pharmacology as it will affect the house officer.

Whilst every effort has been made to make the information within this book as accurate as possible, prescribing advice is frequently altered and knowledge of contra-indications and side-effects may change. We strongly advise that you check up-to-date details on the drug data sheets.

The *British National Formulary* has several introductory pages on general prescribing advice which we also strongly advise you read.

Intravenous drugs

Making up IV drugs

PROBLEM
You are presented with a sealed vial of a drug (in powder form) which is at atmospheric pressure, into which you need to inject 5–10 ml of sterile water, dissolve the drug and withdraw the solution for injection into a patient.

OBJECTIVE
To avoid an embarrassing 'drug shower'.

SOLUTION

1 Most antibiotics and other drugs for IV administration can be dissolved in 5–10 ml of water (see Table 2.2). Start with a 10 ml syringe containing 7–8 ml of 'water for injection' (Fig. 2.1(a)).

2 Introduce the needle into the vial under sterile conditions and aspirate 3–4 ml of air. This creates a vacuum in the vial (Fig. 2.1(b)).

3 With the vial upright release the plunger so that water from the syringe flows into the vial — sucked in by the vacuum. Speed up the process by gently applying pressure to the plunger. If you push too hard you will produce a 'drug shower' (Fig. 2.1(c)).

4 If you have injected all of the water into the vial you will be left with positive pressure therein. It is thus important to aspirate 3–4 ml of air and to apply back pressure to the plunger as you withdraw the needle from the vial.

5 Shake the vial vigorously until the drug has dissolved.

6 Re-introduce needle into the vial and inject 3–4 ml of air. Invert the vial and with the needle tip resting just inside the rubber bung, release the plunger. As a result of the positive pressure in the vial, the dissolved drug will flow into the syringe. Speed up the process by pulling back on the plunger (Fig. 2.1(d)).

7 Once all of the dissolved drug is in the syringe, withdraw the needle. Remember to continue to apply back pressure on the plunger as you do so.

The above process may seem a little laborious but after your first hundred IV administrations you will get used to it! Some people prefer to by-pass the problem of pressure differences by introducing a second small needle (orange) into the vial to dissipate these pressure differences. However if you get used to the above technique it is quicker than opening another needle.

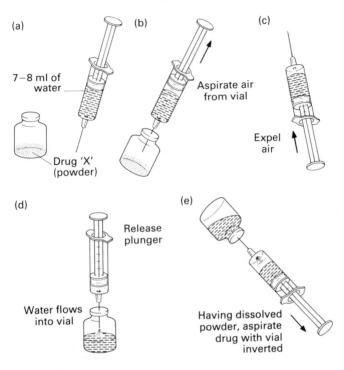

Fig. 2.1 An example of making up an IV drug.

Strictly all IV drugs should be given over at least 3–5 min — in practice they are often given over much shorter times but be limited by the patient's response — several solutions hurt as they are given.

Pharmaceutical incompatibility

If you are required to do regular IV drug rounds you will be tempted to mix drugs to speed up the whole process. This is not to be recommended. There are some drugs which should *never* be mixed (Table 2.1).

Table 2.1 Drugs which should not be mixed with others

> Cimetidine
> Dexamethasone
> Frusemide
> Hydrocortisone
> Metoclopramide
> Parentrovite
> Ranitidine
> Vitamin K
> Gentamicin and other aminoglycosides

Preparation of IV antibiotics

Table 2.2(a) Antibiotics which can *all* be dissolved in 5–10 ml of 'water for injection'

Amoxycillin/ampicillin	250 & 500 mg
Benzylpenicillin	300 & 600 mg
Cephalosporins	Various doses up to 1.5 mg
Chloramphenicol	1 g tds/qds
Flucloxacillin	250 & 500 mg
Piperacillin	1 & 2 g

Table 2.2(b) Antibiotics which need more intricate preparation

Erythromycin	Initially dissolve 1 g vial in 20 ml water for injection. Shake thoroughly and once in solution (may take up to 5 min) dissolve further in at least 250 ml of 0.9% sodium chloride for each 500 mg of drug. Give over 30 min. Dose: 500 mg qds.
Gentamicin	2–5 mg/kg daily in divided doses. See the gentamicin nomogram (see Fig. 2.2). Any dose may be given undiluted over *at least* 3 min.
Metronidazole	Supplied in ready prepared 500 mg IV infusion bags/bottles to be given over 20 min. Dose: 500 mg tds.
Netilmicin	Administer undiluted over *at least* 3 min. Dose: For 50 kg patient: 100 mg bd–100 mg tds. For 90 kg patient: 120 mg tds–180 mg tds. Exercise caution in renal failure.

Table 2.2(b)   (*continued*)

Tobramycin	Dissolve in 100–150 ml 0.9% sodium chloride and give over 20–60 min.
	Dose: 3–5 mg/kg daily (you could use the gentamicin nomogram)
	  For 50 kg patient: 50 mg tds–80 mg tds.
	  For 90 kg patient: 90 mg tds–150 mg tds.
	Caution in renal failure.

Ticarcillin	Dissolve in 20 ml water and give over 3–5 min. Dose: 15–20 g daily, e.g. 5 g tds.

Vancomycin	Initially dissolve in 10 ml water. Then further dissolve
	  in 100–200 ml 5% dextrose or 0.9% sodium chloride and
	  give over *at least* 60 min.
	Dose: 500 mg qds or 1 g bd.

Drug infusions

General information

Around the country there are various types of administration techniques available for intravenous infusions, e.g. various infusion pumps and syringe pumps of several different makes. Worse still, some run at millilitres per hour infusion rates and some run at drops per minute rates. This section contains advice on both systems.

If you are required to use a 'drops per minute' system check in each case whether you are using a 20 *or* 60 drops/ml infusion line. This will be written on the packaging of the tubing. Because this is an important distinction we have clearly indicated, in the case of each drug, which calibre of tubing the data refer to. We have provided Table 2.3 in case you are required for various reasons to convert from drops per minute to millilitres per hour.

Aminophylline

[Please read the introductory pages to this chapter before preparing any infusions.]

Table 2.3 Converting millilitres per hour to drops per minute

ml/h	Drops/min (20 drops/ml giving set)	Drops/min (60 drops/ml giving set)
10	3–4	10
20	7	20
30	10	30
40	13	40
50	17	50
60	20	60
70	23	70
80	27	80
90	30	90
100	33	100

Indications	Reversible airways disease and acute severe asthma.
Forms	**1** 10 ml ampoule containing 250 mg of aminophylline.
	2 2 ml ampoule containing 500 mg of aminophylline.
Diluting agent	5% dextrose or 0.9% sodium chloride.
Giving set	20 drops/ml [*NB*: ignore if using a ml/h system].

Procedure

1 Give a loading dose of 250–500 mg (5 mg/kg) IV over 20 min — omit if patient is already on oral theophylline/ aminophylline or GP has already given a loading dose.

2 Add 500 mg of aminophylline to 500 ml of diluting agent.

Concentration = 1 mg/ml.

3 Run via a pump at a rate equivalent to 500 µg/kg/h, as shown in Table 2.4.

It is often very reassuring to wire the patient up to an ECG monitor during the infusion.

Table 2.4 Infusion of a 1 mg/ml aminophylline solution

Patient's weight (kg)	ml/h rate	drops/min rate
90	45	15
80	40	13
70	35	12
60	30	10
50	25	8
40	20	7

Amiodarone

[Please read the introductory pages to this chapter before preparing any infusions.]

Indications	Useful for most supraventricular and ventricular arrhythmias. Beware of multiple side-effects, including hypotension and pro-arrhythmic effects.

NB: Repeated or continuous infusion via a peripheral line is not to be recommended because it can lead to local pain and inflammation. Therefore use a ***central line***.

Forms	3 ml ampoule containing 150 mg = 50 mg/ml.
Diluting agent	5% dextrose.
Giving set	20 drops/ml [*NB*: ignore if using a ml/h system].

Procedure

The standard dose is 5 mg/kg given between 20 min and 2 h as a dilute solution in 250 ml of 5% dextrose. This may be followed by repeat infusions up to a maximum of 1200 mg in up to 500 ml of diluting agent over 24 h. The steps are as follows:

1 Assess approximate weight of patient.

2 Add required amount of amiodarone to 250 ml of 5% dextrose as shown in Table 2.5.

Table 2.5 Required amount of amiodarone relative to patient's weight

	Weight (kg)					
	40	50	60	70	80	90
Dose required (mg)	200	250	300	350	400	450
No. of millilitres from ampoule	4	5	6	7	8	9

Table 2.6 Amiodarone infusion rate

Length of infusion (min)	No. of drops/min	ml/h
30	165	500
60	84	250
120	42	125

3 Decide on the basis of clinical urgency the length of time over which you wish to give the infusion.

4 Set infusion rate as shown in Table 2.6.

Chlormethiazole

[Please read the introductory pages to this chapter before preparing any infusions.]

The house officer's friend! Very useful for the control of acute alcohol withdrawal and other causes of uncontrollable behaviour. See under The confused patient (Chapter 6).

Procedure

1 Run a bottle of chlormethiazole 0.8% via a pump or 20 drops/ml giving set.

2 The data sheet suggests that rapid control may be achieved by infusing 40–100 ml over 5–10 min. You can achieve this as follows. Set the pump to run at 500 ml/h or 165 drops/min. Leave running at this rate for *5 minutes*. Adjust the rate thereafter depending on patient's response — continue reducing the dose to the minimum necessary to control the patient. Beware of respiratory depression.

3 If infusion is continued, arrange for constant nurse supervision, or place the patient in an ITU or HDU bed.

4 Avoid using as a constant infusion for longer than 12 h if possible.

Dobutamine

Please read the introductory pages to this chapter before preparing any infusions.

The patient should be wired up to an ECG if possible. May be given via a peripheral cannula at a low dosage rate, but preferably via a central line. Requires dilution before use.

Indications	For adults who require inotropic support in the treatment of cardiogenic shock (e.g. due to myocardial infarction, or cardiomyopathies), and septic shock. Dose: between 2.5 and 10 µg/kg/min.
Forms	Dobutrex = 20 ml vial containing 250 mg of dobutamine (12.5 mg/ml).
Diluting agent	0.9% sodium chloride, 5% dextrose, dextrose/saline.
Giving set	60 drops/ml [*NB*: ignore if using a ml/h system].

Procedure

There are various methods of administration available:

• Method A

1 Add 250 mg (20 ml) of dobutamine solution to 30 ml of diluting agent in a 50 ml syringe.

Concentration = 5.0 mg/ml

2 Place 50 ml syringe into syringe driver and run at a rate relative to patient's weight and the desired µg/kg/min rate derived from Table 2.7.

Table 2.7 Infusion rate of a 5.0 mg/ml dobutamine solution

Patient weight (kg)	Required µg/kg/min rate			
	2.5	5	7.5	10
50	1.5	3.0	4.5	6.0
75	2.25	4.5	6.75	9.0
100	3.0	6.0	9.0	12.0

Figures within the table represent ml/h (or drops/min for a 60 drops/ml giving set).

- Method B
1 Add 500 mg (40 ml) of dobutamine to 500 ml of diluting agent. (Withdraw 40 ml of diluting agent to give a final volume of 500 ml.)

Concentration = 1.0 mg/ml.

2 Run via an infusion pump or 60 drops/ml giving set at a rate relative to patient's weight and the desired µg/kg/min rate derived from Table 2.8.

Table 2.8 Infusion rate of a 1.0 mg/ml dobutamine solution

Patient weight (kg)	Required µg/kg/min rate			
	2.5	5	7.5	10
50	8	15	23	30
75	11	23	34	45
100	15	30	45	60

Figures within the table represent ml/h (or drops/min for a 60 drops/ml giving set).

Dopamine
[Please read the introductory pages to this chapter before preparing any infusions.]

| *Indications* | For the correction of poor perfusion, low cardiac output, impending renal failure and shock associated with: myocardial infarction; trauma; endotoxic septicaemia; and heart failure. It is a positive inotropic agent causing generalised vasoconstriction at high dose, but at doses of 5 µg/kg/min and below, the renal vessels are spared, with relative increase in renal blood flow. Dose: between 2.5 and 20 µg/kg/min. |

Never administer via a peripheral line. Always use a *central line*.

Forms	Several are available: **1** 5 ml ampoule containing 800 mg dopamine (= 160 mg/ml). **2** 5 ml ampoule containing 200 mg dopamine (= 40 mg/ml). **3** Pre-prepared infusion bags containing dopamine hydrochloride at various concentrations, viz: 800 µg/ml, 1.6 mg/ml, or 3.2 mg/ml.
Diluting agent	0.9% sodium chloride, 5% dextrose, dextrose/saline.
Giving set	60 drops/ml [*NB*: ignore if using a ml/h system].

Procedure

There are various methods of administration depending on which form of the drug you have available. Avoid large infusion volumes in patients in cardiac failure.

The data given in Tables 2.9–2.11 are based on an 80 kg patient but will suffice for the majority of patients. If your patient is at either extreme of the weight scale, you can calculate the exact infusion rate by this formula:

$$\frac{\text{Infusion rate}}{\text{(ml/h or drops/min)}} = \frac{\text{Wt}(\text{kg} \times \text{A})}{17 \times \text{conc of solution (mg/ml)}}$$

where A is the required µg/kg/min infusion rate.

- Method A (using 800 mg/5 ml ampoules)

1 Transfer 800 mg by aseptic technique to 500 ml of diluting agent.

Concentration = 1.6 mg/ml.

2 Infuse at the required µg/kg/min rate (Table 2.9).

Table 2.9   Infusion rate of a 1.6 mg/ml dopamine solution

	Required µg/kg/min rate					
	2.5	5	7.5	10	15	20
Conc = 1.6 mg/ml	7.5	15	23	30	45	60

Figures within the table represent ml/h (or drops/min for a 60 drops/ml giving set).

- Method B (using 200 mg/5 ml ampoules)

1 Place 200 mg into a 50 ml syringe and add 45 ml of diluting agent to give a final volume of 50 ml.

Concentration = 4.0 mg/ml.

2 Run in a syringe driver at the required µg/kg/min rate as shown in Table 2.10.

Table 2.10   Infusion rate of a 4.0 mg/ml dopamine solution

	Required µg/kg/min rate					
	2.5	5	7.5	10	15	20
Conc = 4.0 mg/ml	3	6	9	12	18	24

Figures within the table represent ml/h (or drops/min for a 60 drops/ml giving set).

- Method C (using ready prepared dopamine infusion bags)
Use them at the required µg/kg/min rate as shown in Table 2.11.

Table 2.11 Infusion rate of various concentrations of dopamine solution

Concentration (mg/ml)	Required µg/kg/min rate						
	2.5	5	7.5	10	15	20	25
0.8	15	30	45	60	90	120	150
1.6	7.5	15	23	30	45	60	75
3.2	4	7.5	11	15	23	30	37

NB: Be sure you use the correct data for the strength of infusion solution you are using. Figures within the table represent ml/h (or drops/min for a 60 drops/ml giving set).

Doxapram

[Please read the introductory pages to this chapter before preparing any infusions.]

Indications	A respiratory stimulant useful when mechanical ventilatory support is inappropriate and in patients with hypercapnic respiratory failure (where oxygen therapy causes a rise in P_{CO_2}) who are becoming drowsy. Only use under expert supervision.
Forms	1 Pre-prepared 500 ml infusion bags at a concentration of 2 mg/ml. 2 5 ml ampoules containing 100 mg of doxapram (= 20 mg/ml).
Diluting agent	5% dextrose.
Giving set	20 drops/ml [*NB*: ignore if using a ml/h system].

Procedure

If using ampoules, add 1000 mg (i.e. 5 ampoules) to 500 ml of diluting agent to give a concentration of 2 mg/ml. Infuse a 2 mg/ml solution at the reducing rate shown in Table 2.12 which is recommended to result in rapid production of a steady state plasma concentration of doxapram:

Table 2.12 Infusion rate of a 2 mg/ml doxapram solution

Time	mg/min	Rate (ml/h)	Rate (drops/min)
From 0–15 min then	4	120	40
From 15–30 min then	3	90	30
From 30–60 min then	2	60	20
60 min onwards	1.5	45	15

Measure ABG hourly during initial period until results have stabilised.

Gentamicin nomogram (Fig. 2.2)

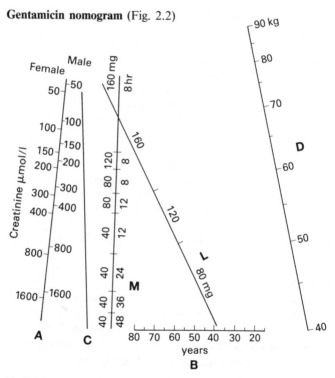

Fig. 2.2 Gentamicin nomogram. A = plasma creatinine level in mmol/l; B = age in years; C = reference line; D = weight in kg; M = dose and frequency; L = loading dose in mg. Note that most laboratories report creatinine in μmol/l (therefore divide by 1000). From Mawer, G. (1974) *Br J Clin Pharmcol* **1** p. 45.

Procedure

1 Join appropriate points on lines **A** and **B** relative to your patient.

2 Then, from the point where your line from **A** to **B** intercepts line **C**, join up with the appropriate point on line D.

3 The point where this line intercepts line **M** gives the dose and frequency, e.g. 40 mg 12 hourly.

4 The point where the same line intercepts line **L** gives you the loading dose.

Note that this nomogram may also be used for tobramycin.

Heparin

Please read the introductory pages to this chapter before preparing any infusions.

Indications	DVT, PE, DIC (controversial), post rtPA thrombolytic therapy, occasionally in unstable angina and after percutaneous transluminal angioplasty.
Forms	Vials containing various numbers of units of heparin. Ensure that you are using heparin for intravenous use.
Diluting agent	0.9% sodium chloride.

Procedure

1 Ensure a baseline clotting result is available.

2 Give a loading dose of 5000 u IV over 5 min.

3 Decide on an initial dosage between 20 000 and 40 000 u per 24 h depending on the size and age of the patient.

How you proceed now will depend on the system used in your hospital for heparin infusions:

If you have syringe drivers that take 50 ml syringes follow Method A.

If you are to use syringe drivers that take 20 ml syringes follow Method B.

- Method A

1 Add the necessary number of units to a 50 ml syringe and make up the final volume to 48 ml with 0.9% sodium chloride.
2 Run via a syringe pump at 2 ml/h. The syringe will thus last 24 h.

or

- Method B

1 Add half the necessary number of units to a 20 ml syringe and make up the final volume to 20 ml with 0.9% sodium chloride.
2 Run via the syringe pump.

The dose reduction is necessary because these syringe drivers normally run over 12 h (= 1.6 ml/h). Check that this is the case.

Aim for a KCCT/PTTK result 1.5–2.5 × control value. Check KCCT/PTTK at 6 h after starting and adjust the infusion rate on the basis of this clotting result as shown in Table 2.13.

Table 2.13 Adjustment of a heparin solution based on the KCCT/PTTK result

KCCT/PTTK ratio	Change in infusion rate
> 7	Stop infusion for 1 h then recommence, reducing rate by 12 000 u/24 h
5.1–7.0	Reduce by 12 000 u/24 h
4.1–5.0	Reduce by 7000 u/24 h
3.1–4.0	Reduce by 2500 u/24 h
2.6–3.0	Reduce by 1200 u/24 h
1.5–2.5	Perfect!
1.2–1.4	Increase by 5000 u/24 h
< 1.2	Increase by 10 000/24 h

After Fennerty, A., Campbell, I.A., Routledge, P.A. (1988) Anticoagulants in venous thromboembolism *Br Med J* 1285–8.

NB: If you experience difficulties in obtaining control, ask for help from the haematologists because there is often an underlying clotting defect which may need special tests to elucidate.

Insulin

[Please read the introductory pages to this chapter before preparing any infusions.]

May be given via IV or subcutaneous routes. The dosage is dependent on the patient's blood sugar levels as measured by ward glucose tests and periodic laboratory checks on blood sugar. Remember the plasma potassium needs assaying regularly in the keto-acidotic patient.

Forms	Use soluble insulin, e.g. Actrapid.
Diluting agent	0.9% sodium chloride.

Procedure 1. IV sliding scale

1 Draw up 50 ml of diluting agent into a 50 ml syringe.

2 Add 50 u of Actrapid (= 1 u/ml).

3 Opinion varies as to the correct rate at which to infuse the insulin. Table 2.14 is an example and you should check whether your seniors find this suitable. Most hospitals now have agreed policies for management of diabetic keto-acidosis.

Table 2.14 Intravenous insulin sliding scale

Ward glucose result	Units insulin/h
0–3	½
3–7	1
7–13	2
13–22	4
> 22	6 and call doctor

Hourly ward glucose recordings are required.

Patients receiving treatment for keto-acidotic hyperglycaemia require simultaneous IV fluids.

If ward glucose > 11 mmol/litre give 0.9% sodium chloride: avoid giving more than 3–4 litres without further discussion with your seniors.

If ward glucose < 11 mmol/litre give 5% dextrose.

Once blood sugar levels are in the normal range, there are no ketones in the urine, and the arterial pH is normal, transfer to subcutaneous doses.

Procedure 2. SC insulin

Subcutaneous sliding scales should not be encouraged. It is better to use SC doses of short-acting insulin at regular intervals with close ward glucose monitoring (at least 4 hourly). To decide how many units to give:

1 Add up the number of IV units of insulin given over the past 12 h.

2 Double this dose to give the total number of units to be used over 24 h.

3 Divide this total dose into a tds dosing schedule.

4 If the ward glucose result rises over 15 mmol/l give two further units of soluble insulin as often as necessary.

5 Adjust the tds dosage each day and when stable convert to a bd regimen (giving the same total dosage over 24 h), using a mixed insulin.

Isoprenaline

[Please read the introductory pages to this chapter before preparing any infusions.]

Indications	Rarely used: only do so if instructed to do so by a senior colleague.
	1 Shock states: dose 0.5–10 µg/min.
	2 Severe bradycardia: dose 1–4 µg/min.
Forms	Ampoules containing either:
	1 200 µg of isoprenaline in 10 ml (20 µg/ml), or
	2 2 mg of isoprenaline in 2 ml (1 mg/ml).
Diluting agent	5% dextrose, dextrose/saline.
Giving set	20 drops/ml [*NB*: ignore if using a ml/h system].

Procedure

1 Add 5 mg of drug to 500 ml of diluting agent.

2 Decide on appropriate μg/min infusion rate depending on clinical situation.

3 The required infusion rate (drops/min or ml/h) is shown in Table 2.15.

Table 2.15 Infusion of a 10 μg/ml isoprenaline solution

Infusion rate	Required dose (μg/min)										
	0.5	1	2	3	4	5	6	7	8	9	10
No. drops/min	1	2	4	6	8	10	12	14	16	18	20
ml/h	3	6	12	18	24	30	36	42	48	54	60

Lignocaine

[Please read the introductory pages to this chapter before preparing any infusions.]

Indications	Treatment of ventricular tachyarrhythmias.
Forms	**1** Ready prepared infusion bags of lignocaine in 5% dextrose at concentrations of 1 mg/ml (i.e. 0.1%) or 2 mg/ml (i.e. 0.2%).
	2 Xylocard: lignocaine hydrochloride powder reconstituted to 200 mg/ml (1 g or 2 g vials). These must be diluted before use as follows. Add 1 g of reconstituted lignocaine to 500 ml of diluting agent. This will give you a 2 mg/ml solution.
	3 Various vials used for local anaesthetic or injection are available but these all contain low concentrations of lignocaine and thus you will need to open several to make up enough lignocaine to provide for a reasonable length of infusion.

NB: Remember that 100 mg = 5 ml of 2% lignocaine.

Diluting agent	0.9% sodium chloride, 5% dextrose, Ringer's solution, dextrans.
Giving set	20 drops/ml [*NB*: ignore if using a ml/h system].

Procedure

1 Give 100 mg as a bolus dose over 2 min.

2 Follow this by a varying infusion rate of: 4 mg/min for 30 min; 2 mg/min for 2 h; and 1 mg/min thereafter.

Thus for a 2 mg/ml (0.2%) lignocaine solution, run via an infusion pump as follows:

30 min at 120 ml/h *or* 40 drops/min.

2 h at 60 ml/h *or* 20 drops/min.

Thereafter, 30 ml/h *or* 10 drops/min.

For a 0.1% (1 mg/ml) solution, double the infusion rates.

Magnesium

[Please read the introductory pages to this chapter before preparing any infusions.]

Indications	Occasionally needed to correct magnesium deficiency resulting from alcoholism, prolonged diarrhoea, long-term IV fluid replacement or diuretic therapy.
Form	Magnesium chloride or sulphate (e.g. 4 mmol magnesium in 2 ml).
Diluting agent	5% dextrose, 0.9% sodium chloride, dextrose/saline.
Giving set	20 drops/min [*NB*: ignore if using a ml/h system].

Procedure

If the patient is able to tolerate an infusion of a litre of fluid, add 35–50 mmol of magnesium to 1 litre of diluting agent and infuse over 12–24 h (= 60 ml/h *or* 20 drops/min).

Alternatively, add 5 g (= 20 mmol) of magnesium sulphate to 50 ml of diluting agent (concentration = 100 mg/ml) and infuse over 3 h (= 17 ml/h or 5 drops/min).

Caution should be exercised in renal failure and heart block.

Nitrates
[Please read the introductory pages to this chapter before preparing any infusions.]

GLYCERYL TRINITRATE

Indications	**1** Congestive cardiac failure. Dose: Initially 20–25 µg/min (= 1.2–1.5 mg/h) reducing to 10 µg/min or increasing in steps of 20–25 µg/min every 15–30 min until clinical improvement is observed — to a maximum of 200 µg/min (= 12 mg/h). **2** Unstable angina. An initial dose of 10 µg/min (= 0.6 mg/h) is recommended with increments of 10 µg/min being made at approximately 30 min intervals as required — to a maximum of 200 µg/min (= 12 mg/h). **3** As an aid to management of bleeding varices — see below under vasopressin infusions.
Forms	Various sized ampoules containing 0.5 mg/ml, 1 mg/ml or 5 mg/ml — some preparations need to be diluted before use.
Diluting agent	0.9% sodium chloride, 5% dextrose.
Giving set	20 drops/ml — preferably use polyethylene apparatus.

Procedure

The procedure you adopt will depend to a large extent on the techniques you have available to you. We have listed two common examples here.

• Example A

1 Add 50 mg of GTN parenteral preparation to a 50 ml syringe and make up final volume to 50 ml with diluting agent.

Concentration = 1 mg/ml.

2 Run via a syringe pump.

3 Commence at 1 mg/h (= 1 ml/h).

4 Insist on hourly BP measurements.

5 Titrate infusion rate against BP and pain. Reduce infusion rate if systolic BP is less than 100 mmHg.

6 Long-term use may make the patient intoxicated.

or

• Example B

1 Add 50 mg of parenteral GTN to 500 ml of diluting agent (withdraw the same volume of diluting agent as volume of parenteral GTN to be added).

Concentration = 100 µg/ml.

2 Infuse at required rate as shown in Table 2.16.

Table 2.16   Infusion rate of a 0.1 mg/ml GTN solution

Dose (µg/min)	ml/h	No. drops/min
10	6	2
20	12	4
30	18	6
40	24	8
50	30	10
100	60	20
200	120	40

ISOSORBIDE DINITRATE

Indications	**1** Congestive cardiac failure of various causes.
	2 Unstable angina pectoris.
	Dose: 1–10 mg/h adjusted according to response.
Forms	**1** 0.1% solution (= 1 mg/ml). Available in 10 ml ampoules (10 mg), 50 ml bottles (50 mg), and 100 ml bottles (100 mg).
	2 0.05% solution (= 500 µg/ml) in a 50 ml bottle.
Diluting agent	0.9% sodium chloride, 5% dextrose.
Giving set	20 drops/ml [*NB*: ignore if using a ml/h system].

Procedure

This depends on the form of solution available.

- Method A (using 0.1% solution)

Add 50 mg of ISDN to diluting agent to give a final volume of 500 ml.

Concentration = 100 µg/ml.

Infuse as shown in Table 2.17.

Table 2.17   Infusion rate of a 100 µg/ml ISDN solution

ISDN (mg/h)	ml/h	Drops/min
1	10	3–4
2	20	7
3	30	10
4	40	13
5	50	17
6	60	20
7	70	23
8	80	27
9	90	30
10	100	33

• Method B (using 0.1% solution)
If you have 100 ml bottles available, add to 400 ml of diluting agent.

Concentration = 200 µg/ml.

Infuse as shown in Table 2.18.

Table 2.18   Infusion rate of a 200 µg/ml ISDN solution

ISDN (mg/h)	ml/h	Drops/min
1	5	1–2
2	10	3
3	15	5
4	20	7
5	25	8
6	30	10
7	35	12
8	40	13
9	45	15
10	50	17

• Method C
If using 0.05% solution, it can be used undiluted.

Concentration = 500 µg/ml.

Infuse as shown in Table 2.19:

Table 2.19   Infusion rate of a 500 µg/ml ISDN solution

ISDN (mg/h)	ml/h	Drops/min
1	2	0.5
2	4	1.5
3	6	2.0
4	8	2.5
5	10	3.0
6	12	4.5
7	14	5.0
8	16	5.5
9	18	6.0
10	20	6.5

Paracetamol overdose — treatment with *N*-acetyl-L-cysteine

Treatment with *N*-acetyl-L-cysteine is indicated if the plasma paracetamol concentration in relation to time after overdosage falls just below or above the 'treatment line' in Fig. 2.3. If there is any doubt about the timing of the overdose, it is now accepted that treatment up to 24 h is safe and almost certainly effective.

If treatment is to be given, there is a standard dosing regimen for Parvolex administration. This drug is given in three stages and at a different concentration at each stage as follows:

First dose: 150 mg/kg in 200 ml 5% dextrose, IV over 15 min.

Second dose: 50 mg/kg in 500 ml 5% dextrose, IV over 4 h.

Third dose: 100 mg/kg in 1000 ml 5% dextrose, IV over 16 h.

Fortunately you don't have to work any of these doses out because the necessary information is given in Table 2.20. This table shows what *volume* of Parvolex to add to each of the volumes of 5% dextrose at each stage relative to the patient's weight.

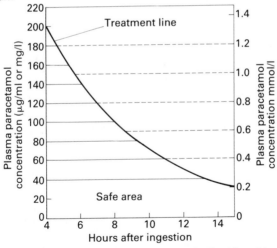

Fig. 2.3 A graph to indicate those patients who should receive *N*-acetyl-L-cysteine. From Prescott, L.F. (1978) *Health Bull* 4 p. 204.

Table 2.20 Amount of Parvolex required at first, second and third dose stages

Body wt (kg)	Dose stage	Parvolex Dose (ml)	Parvolex No. of ampoules	Body wt (kg)	Dose stage	Parvolex Dose (ml)	Parvolex No. of ampoules
40	1st	30	3.0	68	1st	51	5.1
	2nd	10	1.0		2nd	17	1.7
	3rd	20	2.0		3rd	34	3.4
44	1st	33	3.3	72	1st	54	5.4
	2nd	11	1.1		2nd	18	1.8
	3rd	22	2.2		3rd	36	3.6
48	1st	36	3.6	76	1st	57	5.7
	2nd	12	1.2		2nd	19	1.9
	3rd	24	2.4		3rd	38	3.8
52	1st	39	3.9	80	1st	60	6.0
	2nd	13	1.3		2nd	20	2.0
	3rd	26	2.6		3rd	40	4.0
56	1st	42	4.2	84	1st	63	6.3
	2nd	14	1.4		2nd	21	2.1
	3rd	28	2.8		3rd	42	4.2
60	1st	45	4.5	88	1st	66	6.6
	2nd	15	1.5		2nd	22	2.2
	3rd	30	3.0		3rd	44	4.4
64	1st	48	4.8	92	1st	69	6.9
	2nd	16	1.6		2nd	23	2.3
	3rd	32	3.2		3rd	46	4.6

Phenytoin

[Please read the introductory pages to this chapter before preparing any infusions.]

Indications	Status epilepticus, seizures in neurosurgery, ventricular arrhythmia resulting from digoxin toxicity.
Forms	Epanutin Ready Mixed Parenteral (= 5 ml ampoules of phenytoin sodium 50 mg/ml). Total dose of 250 mg.

NB: Do not use if the vial contains a precipitate or becomes hazy. If the vial has been stored in a fridge a precipitate might form — this should dissolve again after the solution is allowed to stand at room temperature and is still suitable for use.

Diluting agent	Continuous infusion should be avoided: the addition of parenteral Epanutin to IV infusion fluids is not recommended because of the likelihood of crystallisation.
Giving set	20 drops/ml [*NB*: ignore if using a ml/h system].

Procedure

1 A loading dose of 10–15 mg/kg should be given. The required volume of drug is shown in Table 2.21.

2 Infuse required volume of drug undiluted at a rate of 60 ml/h (= 20 drops/min for a 20 drop/ml giving set), and monitor ECG and BP.

3 Maintenance doses of about 100 mg should be given by slow IV injection thereafter at intervals of 6 h, adjusted on the basis of plasma concentrations.

Each injection of intravenous phenytoin should be followed by an injection of sterile saline through the same needle or

Table 2.21 Volume of phenytoin required relative to patient's weight

Patient wt (kg)	Amount of drug required (mg)	Vol of drug required (ml)
50	750	15
55	825	16.5
60	900	18
65	975	19.5
70	1050	21
75	1125	22.5
80	1200	24
85	1275	25.5

catheter to avoid local venous irritation due to the alkalinity of the solution.

Potassium

[Please read the introductory pages to this chapter before preparing any infusions.]

NB: There are many varying ideas about the maximum concentration and rate of infusion of potassium. We present here information derived from our own experiences but recommend that you check this with your seniors to see that they feel it is suitable.

Potassium may be given IV with caution if insufficient amounts can be taken by mouth. Intravenous administration is indicated if the potassium level is less than 3.0 mmol/l. If possible use a central line.

Forms	**1** Ready prepared fluid infusion bags containing various concentrations of potassium.
	2 Potassium chloride strong solution (= 10 ml ampoules containing 20 mmol of potassium chloride). This needs dilution with not less than 50 times its own volume of the diluting agent of your choice.
Giving set	Any of your choice.

Procedure

Never infuse more than 20 mmol/h and rarely at a concentration of more than 80 mmol/l.

Use a concentration of 40 mmol/l if the potassium level is between 2.5 and 3.0 mmol/l.

Use up to 80 mmol/l if potassium is less than 2.5 mmol/l.

Repeated measurements of plasma potassium are required, as often as 2 hourly in the keto-acidotic patient and more frequently after starting treatment for hyperosmolar non-ketotic hyperglycaemia. Remember that rapid changes in potassium may be more hazardous than an initially low chronic value.

Salbutamol
[Please read the introductory pages to this chapter before preparing any infusion.]

Indications	Acute severe asthma and other causes of reversible airways obstruction.
Dose	In status asthmaticus: 5–20 µg/min. Start at 5 µg/min and adjust on the basis of clinical response.
Form	5 ml ampoules containing salbutamol at 1 mg/ml.
Diluting agent	5% dextrose, 0.9% sodium chloride.
Giving set	20 drops/ml [*NB*: ignore if using a ml/h system].

Procedure

1 Add 5 mg of parenteral salbutamol to 500 ml of diluting agent.

Concentration = 10 µg/ml.

2 Run through a pump according to the required µg/min rate as shown in Table 2.22.

Table 2.22 Infusion of a 10 µg/ml salbutamol solution

µg/min	ml/h	Drops/min
5	30	10
10	60	20
15	90	30
20	120	40

NB: Beware of hypokalaemia.

Terbutaline

[Please read the introductory pages to this chapter before preparing infusion.]

Indications	As for salbutamol.
Dose	1.5–5 µg/min over 8–10 h.
Forms	1 or 5 ml ampoules of terbutaline sulphate at 0.5 mg/ml.
Diluting agent	5% dextrose, 0.9% sodium chloride, dextrose/saline.
Giving set	20 drops/ml [*NB*: ignore if using a ml/h system.]

Procedure

1 Add 5 ml of terbutaline (2.5 mg) to 500 ml of diluting agent.

Concentration = 5 µg/ml.

2 Run via a pump at a rate as shown in Table 2.23.

Table 2.23 Infusion rate of a 5 µg/ml terbutaline solution

µg/min	ml/h	Drops/min
1.5	18	6
2	24	8
3	36	12
4	48	16
5	60	20

Start at lower dose and adjust according to response.

Thiamine

[Please read the introductory pages to this chapter before preparing any infusions.]

Indications	Treatment of deficiency of vitamin B complex and C vitamins, in particular that encountered: **1** In association with alcoholism.

2 In peripheral neuritis, associated with malabsorption syndromes or alcoholism.
3 Postoperatively and following severe acute illness in the elderly.

In practical terms, you will be using thiamine replacement for the prevention of Wernicke's encephalopathy in chronic alcoholics.

Forms	Several are available. Most commonly Parentrovite which comes in the form of two ampoules which must be mixed thoroughly just prior to use. There are IV and intramuscular preparations which must not be confused. They come in similar bottles so *be careful*.
Diluting agent	0.9% sodium chloride or 5% dextrose.
Giving set	20 drops/ml.

Procedure
Mix contents of vials 1 and 2 and add to at least 100 ml of diluting agent. Infuse over 0.5–1 h.

Thrombolytic therapy
This is a rapidly changing area of medicine and you should check with your registrar which type of thromolytic is in vogue at your hospital.

Indications	**1** Convincing history of myocardial infarction within the last 24 h, preferably within the last 6 h. **2** ECG changes: 2 mm ST elevation in the precordial leads *or* 1 mm ST elevation in the limb leads.

Contra-indications *(most of these are relative)*	CVA in the past 3 months
	GI bleed in the past 3 months
	Known or suspected active peptic ulceration
	Recent prolonged cardiopulmonary resuscitation
	Major hepatic/renal disease
	Bleeding diathesis
	Surgery within the last 10 days
	Aortic aneurysm
	Possible pregnancy
	Diabetic proliferative retinopathy
	Any recently inserted central or arterial line
	Hypertension, i.e. systolic greater than 200 mmHg, diastolic greater than 110 mmHg.
	Oral anticoagulants
	Known terminal disease
	Menstruation
	Bacterial endocarditis
Forms	Streptokinase powder for reconstitution, various units/bottle.
	Alteplase (rtPA) powder for reconstitution. 20 mg/vial or 50 mg/vial.
	Anistreplase (APSAC) powder for reconstitution. 30 u/vial.
Diluting agent	0.9% sodium chloride.
Giving set	20 drops/ml [*NB*: ignore if using a ml/h system].

Procedure

1 *Don't forget aspirin.*

2 Decide which drug you are to use. If you usually use streptokinase or anistreplase as first line, these should be avoided if the patient has had either drug in the past 6 months.

Streptokinase Dissolve 1 500 000 u of streptokinase with 10–20 ml of sodium chloride — this can take quite some time and froths endlessly. Add the dissolved drug to 0.9% sodium chloride to give a final volume of 100 ml. Run via a pump at 100 ml/h *or* at 33 drops/min.

Alteplase (rtPA) Dissolve a total of 100 mg in 100 ml diluting agent. Give a 10 mg bolus dose; then 50 mg in 50 ml over the next hour (= 50 ml/h or 16 drops/min); and then 40 mg in 100–250 ml over 2 h (50–125 ml/h). See drug data sheet for recommendations on heparin infusions.

Anistreplase Dissolve as per data sheet, giving 30 u over 4–5 min.

NB: When dissolving aim the diluent against the side of the vial and do not shake — otherwise it froths endlessly.

Avoid vascular puncture during the active phase of thrombolysis, which extends for 30 min after the end of the infusion of anistreplase, and for 6 h after streptokinase: take blood beforehand.

Vasopressin
[Please read the introductory pages to this chapter before preparing any infusions.]

Indications	Some gastrointestinal units use a combination of vasopressin and GTN infusions in the acute management of variceal haemorrhage.
Forms	1 ml ampoules of Pitressin 20 u/ml.
Diluting agent	5% dextrose.
Giving set	20 drops/ml [*NB*: ignore if using a ml/h system].

Procedure

1 Add 5 ampoules (= 100 u) to 500 ml of 5% dextrose.

2 Give 20 units in 15 min by running the infusion at 400 ml/h *or* 135 drops/min.

3 Slow the infusion down to 10 u/h by adjusting the rate of infusion to 50 ml/h or 17 drops/min.

4 If the haemorrhage has not stopped within 1–2 h, double the infusion rate.

5 If the patient's condition remains stable on 10 u/h for the next 24 h, gradually reduce dose until able to stop.

A GTN infusion should always be run at the same time to offset the effects of widespread vasoconstriction. This is important for the coronary vessels — see above under Nitrate infusions.

NB: Beware of hypotension: stop GTN if systolic BP drops below 100 mmHg.

Oral drugs

Angiotensin converting enzyme inhibitors

This group of drugs has revolutionised the life of patients with cardiac failure. They should be used with caution since they can initially lower the BP dramatically, particularly if the plasma sodium concentration is less than 130 mmol/l. Many physicians bring their more severely ill patients into hospital to commence these drugs.

Stop any potassium-sparing diuretics because ACE inhibitors promote potassium retention (e.g. change Frumil to frusemide). Consider reducing diuretics 2 days before introducing ACE inhibitors (particularly if they have a high urea or hyponatraemia). This is often not possible in those with gross cardiac failure. Keep a close eye on the U & E results over the first few days since these drugs can precipitate renal failure particularly in patients with bilateral renal artery stenosis.

Procedure

1 Make sure that the plasma sodium concentration is greater than 130 mmol/l and that systolic BP is greater than 100 mmHg. If it is lower then discuss further management with your registrar.

2 Give 6.25 mg of captopril as a test dose at night and assess the BP hourly for 4 h.

3 If the BP does not fall precipitously (e.g. systolic BP below 90 mmHg) then this dose can be repeated the next morning.

Doses can be increased according to tolerance and response (see the *British National Formulary* for guidelines).

Amiodarone

Patients who have *not* received IV loading doses need to be started on an oral loading regimen, because of the extensive half-life of this drug. Proceed as follows:

200 mg tds for 1 week

200 mg bd for 1 week

200 mg daily thereafter — or less if possible.

Check the therapeutic level at this stage — see under therapeutic drug level monitoring (Chapter 2).

Analgesia

Given that one of our most important functions as doctors is to control and minimise pain and suffering, we, as juniors, are sadly incompetent at this task. There is a bewildering number of preparations available and patients show an equally bewildering range of responses to these many formulations.

PRACTICAL POINTS

1 Ask an experienced staff nurse or sister what they would recommend for your patient. They will have been managing pain infinitely longer than you have and they will also know what is available in your hospital.

2 Analgesics are always more effective if used prophylactically, rather than allowing pain to develop. Thus if your patient is frequently requesting analgesia, try regular doses of mild analgesics before moving on to a stronger preparation.

3 There are often designated pain control specialists available for advice. Their interest is in the effective management of chronic or severe acute pain symptoms and it is our experience that they are keen to be involved earlier rather than later. Don't be reserved or embarrassed about your lack of knowledge — they know you know nothing about pain management.

4 Remember that all analgesics have side-effects and these must, to a degree, influence your choice.

5 If your patient is experiencing pain that warrants IV or IM opiates, you should convert to oral administration as soon as possible.

6 If you are to start someone on oral morphine for chronic pain, it is preferable to use slow-release preparations such as MST Continus. Begin with 20 mg bd if no other analgesic has been used previously; but if replacing a weaker opioid (e.g. Co-dydramol) begin with 20–30 mg bd. If the patient experiences pain which develops despite regular analgesic treatment, increase the next dose by 10 mg and give 10 mg of morphine elixir to cover the interim period. Instruct the patient to request further analgesia as the need arises (many patients prefer to 'grin and bear it'). Keep assessing the effectiveness of your prescription. As a general principle, increase dosage not frequency.

7 You may want to start using a diamorphine pump on terminally ill patients. We outline here an example of a SC infusion using a Graseby pump. Proceed as follows: Add 9 ml of water for injection plus 10 mg of diamorphine plus or minus 5–10 mg of haloperidol plus 800–1200 µg of hyoscine. Run at 2 mm/h for 24 h. Adjust on the basis of successful symptom control.

8 It is useful when choosing an analgesic to divide pain into *mild*, *moderate* and *severe* categories and to become familiar with two or three preparations for each degree of pain. Tables 2.24 and 2.25 are designed to help clarify the relevant potencies of commonly used analgesics to help you choose one in specific conditions. It is worth remembering that several pain syndromes have specific analgesic treatments.

Equivalents

1 One oral dose of diamorphine equals half an IM dose of diamorphine.

2 One oral dose of morphine equals one-quarter to one-third of an IM dose of diamorphine.

3 One oral dose of morphine equals half an IM dose of morphine.

If you are converting a patient from regular oral morphine to MST continus, add the total amount given in 24 h and then halve the amount. Give this dose of MST bd.

Table 2.24 Categories of analgesic

Pain intensity	Analgesic
Mild	Paracetamol
	NSAID (e.g. ibuprofen, aspirin)
Moderate	NSAID (e.g. diclofenac)
	Combination formulations:
	Codeine phosphate and paracetamol (e.g. Co-codamol)
	Paracetamol and dextropropoxyphene (e.g. Co-proxamol)
	Paracetamol and dihydrocodeine (e.g. Co-dydramol)
	Papaveretum and aspirin
	Narcotics:
	Codeine
	Dihydrocodeine
	Dextropropoxyphene
	Buprenorphine, pentazocine
Severe	Morphine
	Diamorphine
	Pethidine
	Papaveretum
	Dextromoramide

Remember to think of non-analgesic treatment of pain such as TENS, e.g. in chronic osteoporotic back pain; carbamazepine for diabetic neuropathy and trigeminal neuralgia; or meprobamate for phantom limb pain.

Table 2.25 Appropriate analgesics for clinical problems

Simple headache	Paracetamol (po)
Sciatic pain	
Mild	Co-proxamol, Co-dydramol, NSAID (po)
Severe	Strong NSAID, e.g. diclofenac or naproxen
Postoperative pain	
Mild	Dihydrocodeine, Co-dydramol (po), buprenorphine (SL)
Severe	Pethidine or papaveretum (IM/po)
Acute abdominal pain	Pethidine or papaveretum (IM) other than renal colic
Colicky abdominal pain	Buscopan (IM/po)
Renal colic	Diclofenac (IM/po)
Acute MI	Morphine or diamorphine (IV)
Dysmenorrhoea	Mefenamic acid (po)
Bone pain from metastases	Narcotic analgesic and indomethacin (po)
Pleuritic/pericardial chest pain	Indomethacin or other NSAID (po)

Oral anticoagulation therapy

Drug interactions with warfarin are frequent and can be serious. When starting or stopping treatment check the *British National Formulary*.

If long-term anticoagulation is intended, commence oral warfarin whilst continuing IV heparin. There is much debate as to when to start loading with warfarin — check the policy of your firm. There are also many suggested protocols and it is often difficult to know what the continuation dose should be once loading is complete. This is a suggested regimen:

1 Obtain a baseline clotting result.

2 Days 1 and 2, give 10 mg of warfarin at 1800 h.

3 Day 3. Check INR. The aim is to keep the INR between 2 and 4.5 depending on the clinical indication (Table 2.26). The dose to give on day 3 and subsequent maintenance dosages are shown in Table 2.27.

Table 2.26 Recommended therapeutic ranges for the INR

	International Normalised Ratio
Prophylaxis of DVT	2–2.5
Treatment of DVT, PE, TIAs	2–3
Prosthetic mechanical heart valves	3–4.5

Table 2.27 Alteration of warfarin dose based on the INR result

	International Normalised Ratio						
	< 2	2	2.5	2.9	3.3	3.6	4.1
3rd dose (mg)	10	5	4	3	2	0.5	0
Maintenance	> 6	5.5	4.5	4	3.5	3	*

*Miss a dose: give 1–2 mg next day unless INR is still > 4 in which case it is advisable to miss two doses.
After Fennerty, A. *et al.* (1984) *Br Med J* p. 1268.

You will frequently be presented with INR results above the therapeutic range. Table 2.28 is a summary of suitable approaches to management according to the patient's clinical state, as recommended by the British Society for Haematology.

Table 2.28 Recommended management of abnormally high INR results and/or haemorrhage in patients on warfarin

INR 4.5–7 without haemorrhage	Withhold warfarin for one or more days according to the INR
INR > 7 without haemorrhage	Withhold warfarin and consider giving vitamin K — 500 µg by slow IV injection
Mild haemorrhage	Withhold warfarin for one or more days and consider giving vitamin K. If this bleeding occurs at therapeutic levels find the cause (i.e. site etc.)
INR > 2 with life-threatening haemorrhage	Give vitamin K 5 mg by slow IV injection and clotting factor concentrates or FFP 1 litre

NB: Vitamin K will take up to 12 h to act and will prevent oral anticoagulants from acting for several days or even weeks — therefore weigh up the decision before using.

Chlormethiazole

Alcohol withdrawal is common as are other causes of disturbed behaviour. It may be possible to control this behaviour without resorting to IV sedatives. If oral chlormethiazole is the drug of choice it should be given as a reducing course. For IV administration see above under Drug infusions. See under The confused patient (Chapter 6) before using any drugs to control an excited patient.

Suggested protocol

Initial dose	2–4 capsules repeated after 3–4 h if necessary
Day 1	(i.e. first 24 h) 3 tabs qds
Day 2	2 tabs qds
Day 3	2 tabs tds
Day 4	2 tabs bd
Day 5	1 tab bd
Day 6	1 nocte then stop

Give half of these doses for a patient with mild liver failure. It is best to avoid this drug in patients with more severe liver failure.

Digitalisation

Opinion varies as to the best protocol for rapid digitalisation. The following is that recommended by the manufacturers of Lanoxin:

1 Check urea and electrolyte results — hypokalaemia sensitizes the myocardium to the cardiac glycosides.

2 Give 0.5 mg of oral digoxin 6 *hourly* until a therapeutic result is obtained. Usually 2–4 doses are sufficient.

3 Maintenance dosage is 0.125–0.25 mg daily for patients with relatively normal renal function. In the elderly 0.0625–0.125 mg/day is usually sufficient.

4 Digoxin requires monitoring of levels after 7 days — see below under Therapeutic drug level monitoring.

Beware of the following interactions with digoxin: quinidine, quinine, amiodarone, verapamil; and reduce the dose accordingly. Watch out for drugs or conditions causing hypokalaemia.

Laxatives

Inactivity, opiate analgesics, drugs with anti-cholinergic side-effects and hospital food all tend to lead to constipation. Many patients thus require laxatives during their stay. It is useful to write most patients up for prn laxatives, e.g. senna 2 tabs prn or Milpar 10 ml prn. Different hospitals will have different preferences — find out what the local preference is in your hospital.

There is a growing move away from the use of lactulose because of questionable efficacy and expense (Lewis and Bretherton (1991) *The Pharmaceutical Journal*, May 4) and a greater belief in the use of senna.

It is worth remembering that ispaghula husk (e.g. Fybogel, Regulan) does not work well on a prn basis and is significantly more expensive than senna or Milpar.

If constipation continues and the patient is otherwise well, it is worth trying: (a) regular laxatives — e.g. senna 2 tabs bd and Milpar 20 ml bd; or (b) glycerine suppositories; or (c) phosphate enemas. If still unsuccessful, consider further investigation.

In the elderly, danthron has been found to be very successful on a prn basis (Lewis and Bretherton 1991), and it is also economical. It should however be avoided in the incontinent patient because of the development of contact rashes around the arms.

Night sedation

Most patients find it difficult to sleep in hospital. You should be aware of clinical situations which preclude the prescription of night sedatives (e.g. acute asthma or hepatic encephalopathy). However you will find in practice that the majority of patients *are* written up for temazepam 10–20 mg nocte. If you don't you will find yourself being woken up to prescribe a sleeping tablet to help a patient sleep!

Oral rehydration

Oral rehydration should be employed for all patients with mild to moderate dehydration following persistent diarrhoea. There are numerous preparations available — the type doesn't really matter.

Give 50 ml/kg in the first 4 h (= 3.5 litres for a 70 kg patient) followed by a maintenance dose of 100 ml/kg daily until the diarrhoea stops (= 7 litres per day for a 70 kg patient). You will rarely if ever get near to this volume but you should ensure that the patient receives enough oral fluid to replace the volume lost in the stool. If not you will need to start IV fluid replacement.

Prednisolone reducing course

Large doses of steroids are often used in acute asthmatic attacks, and less often in a variety of other conditions. Opinion varies as to how quickly they should be reduced and thus many protocols are used. The majority of physicians favour a slow reduction in dosage over approximately 3 weeks for steroid courses used in the acute asthmatic. However (to make the subject even more confusing) there is a growing trend towards giving a 2–4 week course of high-dose steroids and then stopping suddenly without resorting to a reducing course. It is felt that this length of treatment does not result in significant inhibition of the adrenopituitary system. This is a rapidly changing field of medicine and we recommend that you check the latest recommendations of the British Thoracic Society. We present here a sample 'reducing course' in case this is what you are required to prescribe.

Suggested protocol: Start at 40 mg/day. When the patient is improving clinically it may be possible to commence a reduction in dosage, e.g.:

Day 1–3   30 mg/day
Day 4–7   25 mg/day
Day 8–11   20 mg/day
Day 12–14   15 mg/day
Day 15–17   10 mg/day
Day 18–21   5 mg daily then stop.

Theophylline prediction program

There are various computer prediction programs available to assess the correct dosage of theophylline for your patients. The pharmacodynamics and pharmacokinetics of the theophyllines are such that they are affected by a wide variety of variables. The list below indicates the information generally required by the pharmacist to use the programs.

Remember to check the plasma theophylline/aminophylline level of all of your patients at least once during their stay.

Patient's characteristics
Name, age, sex, weight, height.

Other factors
Congestive cardiac failure, pulmonary oedema, COAD, hepatic cirrhosis, smoker?
Is the patient on: barbiturates, erythromycin, cimetidine, benzodiazepines, tricyclics, ciprofloxacin?

Drug details
Theophylline/aminophylline dose.
Dosing interval.
Date and time of last dose.
Number of doses if commenced recently.

General pharmacology information

Penicillin allergy

Three to five per cent of the population are hypersensitive to penicillins: there is also cross-reactivity to cephalosporins in about 10% of those sensitive to penicillins. Before labelling somebody as 'penicillin allergic', ascertain exactly what the patient means because often they have had an upset stomach rather than a true allergic reaction. If they have had a rash you must presume that this represents an allergy. In life-threatening situations (e.g. meningococcal meningitis) penicillins will often be used even if the patient is known to be allergic. In normal situations you should look for alternative drugs — the choice will depend on the clinical situation, so discuss this with your registrar.

NB: When you are giving penicillin-derived antibiotics to patients unknown to you, *always* ask them if they are penicillin-allergic prior to giving the antibiotic, this question may have been omitted from the original checking procedure.

Which dressing?

Most house officers have little if any idea about wound management. Nurses normally make the decision about which dressing to use but you will be called upon to prescribe these dressings. If you or the nurses are having problems, there are designated wound care specialists in most hospitals who are always keen to help; remember that the nurses and wound care specialists not only know more than you on this subject, they also know more than most of your seniors (although your seniors may not agree that this is the case!).

Table 2.29 explains which dressings are suitable for various wound types and we have listed examples of each type of dressing to at least cushion your ignorance. There are

Table 2.29 Dressing selection for different types of wound

Type of wound	Deep		Shallow	
	Low exudate	Heavy/moderate exudate	Low exudate	Heavy/moderate exudate
Epithelialisation Final stage of healing, pink/white tissue is very fragile	Epithelialising wounds do not have exudate. Use either:		1 Semipermeable film 2 Hydrocolloid	
Granulating Wound is healing, appears red and will bleed easily	1 Hydrocolloid 2 Hydrogel 3 Foam (silastic)	1 Foam (silastic) 2 Alginate	1 Hydrocolloid 2 Hydrogel sheet 2 Semipermeable film	1 Alginate (heavy) 2 Allevyn foam (moderate)
Infected Indicated by clinical signs—pain, erythema, oedema — *not* bacteria	1 Hydrogel	1 Alginate 2 Zerogel	1 Alginate 2 Hydrogel	1 Zerogel 2 Alginate
Sloughy Yellow dead tissue. Remove to allow granulation. Do not confuse with fascia	1 Hydrogel 2 Hydrocolloid 3 Zerogel	1 Alginate rope	1 Hydrocolloid 2 Hydrogel	1 Alginate 2 Zerogel
Necrotic Brown/black dead tissue. Must be removed to allow granulation	Not applicable		1 Mechanical debridement 2 Enzymes 3 Hydrogels	

NB: Each wound is a combination of several different types of tissue—more than one type of dressing may be needed.
Reproduced with the permission of Charing Cross Hospital Infection Control Department.

multiple brands of these dressings, examples of which are as follows:

Dressing type	Brand name
Semipermeable membrane	Tegaderm, Opsite, Bioclusive
Hydrocolloids	Granuflex
Hydrogels	Scherisorb, Geliperm, Vigilon
Foam	Silastic, Lyofoam
Alginates	Sorbsan, Kaltostat
Zerogels	Debrisan, Iodosorb
Enzymes	Varidase
Charcoal	Actisorb, Lyofoam C

Be particularly cautious about prescribing Eusol which retains favour among many senior colleagues but has been shown repeatedly to do more harm than good; discuss this with your wound care specialist.

Therapeutic drug level monitoring

Table 2.30 Therapeutic drug level monitoring

Drug	Time to steady state	Sampling times	Therapeutic range	Information
Amiodarone	Up to 1 month	Any time after steady state achieved	0.6–2.5 mg/l	
Carbamazepine	> 2 weeks when initiating therapy	Peak—3 h post-dose Trough[a]	Multiple therapy: 4-8 mg/l Single therapy: 8–12 mg/l	Induces its own metabolism Changes in dosage during chronic therapy take approximately 1 week to produce an effect
Cyclosporin	48 h	Trough[a]	60–180 µg/l	Peak levels rarely recorded

Table 2.30 (*continued*)

Drug	Time to steady state	Sampling times	Therapeutic range	Information
Digoxin	7 days with normal renal function	At least 6 h post-dose Note time of last dose	0.8–2 µg/l	Must monitor U & E closely as toxicity is potentiated by low K^+ and Mg^{++} or high Ca^{++}
Gentamicin and tobramycin	12–24 h (~3 doses) depending on renal function	Peak—1 h post-dose Trough[a]	Peak 5–10 mg/l Trough[a] <2 mg/l	Do not take blood via a central line because of adsorption on the line Watch renal function
Lithium	4–5 days minimum	12–24 h post-dose	0.5–1.5 mmol/l or 4–11 mg/l	Levels should be checked at least 3 monthly
Phenobarbitone	10–25 days no loading 3–4 days with loading	8–12 h post-dose	20–35 µg/l	Induces its own metabolism
Phenytoin	5–15 days no loading	IV peak 2–4 h post-dose Oral peak 3–9 h post-dose Trough[a]	10–20 mg/l	In general the trough conc. is measured. Enzyme inducer
Theophylline	40 h no loading	IV peak 30 min after loading dose. Oral peak 2 h after liquid formulation, 4–6 h after sustained-release preparation	10–20 mg/l	Aminophylline is metabolised to theophylline so there is no such thing as an aminophylline level

Table 2.30 (*continued*)

Drug	Time to steady state	Sampling times	Therapeutic range	Information
Sodium valproate	30–85 h	Peak 1–3 h post-dose Trough[a]	50–115 mg/l	LFTs at least every 6 months
Vancomycin	32 h	Peak 1 h post-dose Trough[a]	Peak 25–40 mg/l Trough[a] 1–3 mg/l	Watch renal function

[a] Trough levels are all estimated immediately pre-dose; 5 ml of clotted blood is usually ample.

Intravenous fluid regimens

There are endless occasions on which you will be required to write-up a patient for IV fluids. There are likewise many regimens available and it is easy to become confused by the potential complexities. However, as a general rule: a patient who is not eating or drinking requires approximately 2–3 litres of fluid over 24 h. Depending on the U & E results s/he is also likely to need at least 60 mmol of potassium in 24 h. Thus a standard regimen as follows will suffice with surprising regularity:

> 1 litre 0.9% sodium chloride + 20 mmol KCl over 8 h
> 1 litre 5% dextrose + 20 mmol KCl over 8 h
> 1 litre 5% dextrose + 20 mmol KCl over 8 h

This regimen must be altered in:
1 Postoperative patients who should not routinely be given potassium supplementation in the first 36 h.
2 Excessive losses from the gastrointestinal tract in the form of vomiting or diarrhoea should be replaced litre for litre with 0.9% sodium chloride, in addition to the standard regimen.
3 Patients with hepatic failure or varices should *not* be given 0.9% sodium chloride. Stick to dextrose. They will probably also be fluid restricted.

4 In acute renal failure or the polyuric phase of chronic renal failure, replace the previous day's output plus 500 ml with no potassium.

5 In LVF/CCF avoid IV fluids wherever possible.

6 Patients with diabetic pre-coma or coma require several litres of IV fluids initially. Check what your hospital's diabetic keto-acidosis policy is. We have presented a suitable protocol here:

- first half an hour: 1 litre 0.9% sodium chloride
- next 1 hour: 1 litre 0.9% sodium chloride + 20 mmol potassium chloride
- next 2 hours: 1 litre 0.9% sodium chloride + 20 mmol potassium chloride
- next 3 hours: 1 litre 0.9% sodium chloride + 20 mmol potassium chloride
- next 4 hours: 1 litre 0.9% sodium chloride + 20 mmol potassium chloride
- next 5 hours: 1 litre 0.9% sodium chloride + 20 mmol potassium chloride.

Check plasma potassium level 2 hourly initially — more frequently if dealing with hyperosmolar non-ketotic hyperglycaemia.

7 Patients with hyponatraemia rarely need saline. They are much more likely to require fluid restriction; discuss this with your seniors.

Other points

Check U & E results at least daily.

If U & E results suggest that more potassium is required than is provided for by the standard regimen, see under Potassium supplementation.

Beware of writing-up fluids on elderly patients who are unknown to you without assessing a recent U & E result.

Oxygen administration

Respiratory rate is altered in response to the level of carbon dioxide in the blood. This normal physiological mechanism is sometimes lost in patients with COAD who instead depend on hypoxia to maintain an adequate respiratory drive. It is thus important not to remove this hypoxic drive when giving such patients oxygen. To this end, start all patients with COAD on 24% oxygen and assess their response 1 h after starting, by repeating the arterial blood gas estimation. If 24% oxygen has not raised the blood oxygen above 8.0 kPa try 28% oxygen. Repeat the blood gas estimation in 1 h and be guided by the carbon dioxide result — if it is rising this indicates a decreasing respiratory effort limiting your ability to increase the oxygen further. Beware if the $P\text{CO}_2$ rises more than 1.5 kPa from previous reading or rises above 8.0 kPa. Discuss further plans with your seniors. If the $P\text{O}_2$ cannot be improved without a rise in $P\text{CO}_2$ you may have to consider mechanical ventilation or a respiratory stimulant such as doxapram.

Patients without carbon dioxide retention who need oxygen may safely and correctly be given unrestricted oxygen by face mask. This rarely achieves more than 50–60% without an anaesthetic face mask. If using controlled percentage oxygen masks (e.g. Ventimask):

24% = 2 litres/min
28% = 4 litres/min
35% = 8 litres/min
40% = 10 litres/min
60% = 15 litres/min.

Tetanus prophylaxis

You will have to consider the need for tetanus prophylaxis in a wide range of patients with various types of injuries and cuts. Table 2.31 is intended as a guide.

Table 2.31 Tetanus prophylaxis

	Treatment required	
Patient's immunity status	Recent clean wound	Wound 6 h old, contaminated or deeply penetrating
Immunised. Booster within past 1 year	Nil	Nil
Immunised. Booster within past 5 years	Nil	TTB
Immunised. Booster within past 10 years	TTB	HT Ig + TTB
Not immunised or status unknown	HT Ig + tetanus full course	HT Ig + tetanus full course

TTB = tetanus toxoid booster; HT Ig = human tetanus immunoglobulin. Tetanus full course consists of three doses of 0.5 ml of adsorbed tetanus vaccine by IM or SC injection, with intervals of 1 month between doses.

Surface area nomogram: body surface area of adults and children

A nomogram to determine the body surface area of adults and children from their height and weight is given in Fig. 2.4. To use this nomogram, a ruler is aligned with the height and weight on the two lateral axes. The point at which the centre line is intercepted gives the corresponding value for surface area.

The practical formulary

In an endeavour to reduce the need to carry endless texts in your already loaded pockets we have listed in Table 2.32 the commonest prescriptions used in everyday ward work. You should, however, refer to the current volume of the *British National Formulary* for more detailed prescribing instructions.

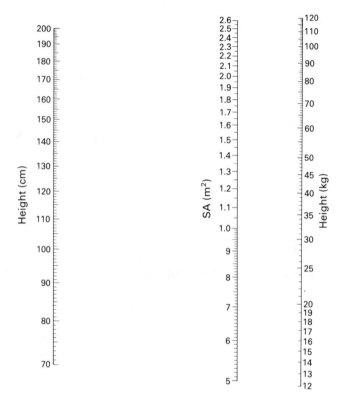

Fig. 2.4 Surface area nomogram. SA = surface area. From Haycock, G.B., Schwartz, G.J. & Wisotsky, D.H. (1978) Geometric method for measuring body surface area: a weight formula validated in infants, children and adults. *J Pediatr* **93** 62–66.

Table 2.32 Prescribing information (adult) for commonly used drugs

Drug	Route	Dose	Frequency
Acetylcysteine	See under Drug infusions — Paracetamol overdose		
Aldomet	See methyldopa		
Alteplase	See under Drug infusions — Thrombolytic therapy		
Alimix	See cisapride		

Table 2.32 (*continued*)

Drug	Route	Dose	Frequency
Aluminium hydroxide	po	1–2 tabs, chewed	qds
		5–10 ml	qds
Amiloride	po	5–20 mg	od
Aminophylline	See under Drug infusions		
Amiodarone	See under Oral drugs and Drug infusions		
Amitriptyline	po	50–75 mg	Nocte. Increase to a maximum of 200 mg/day
Amlodipine	po	5–10 mg	od
Amoxycillin	po/IV	250–500 mg	tds
Ampicillin	po/IV	500 mg	qds
Anistreplase	See under Thrombolytic therapy		
Aspirin	po	300–900 mg	4 hourly; maximum 4 g/day; with food. Lower doses for an antiplatelet effect (e.g. 75 mg od)
Atenolol			
Hypertension	po	50–100 mg	od
Angina	po	100 mg	od
Atrovent	See ipratropium bromide		
Becloforte	Inhaler	2 puffs	bd
		1 puff	qds
Beclomethasone	See Becotide/Becloforte		
Becotide 50	Inhaler	4 puffs	bd
		2 puffs	tds/qds
Becotide 100	Inhaler	2 puffs	bd
		1 puff	tds/qds
Bendrofluazide	po	2.5–5.0 mg	od
Bismuth chelate	po	10 ml (2 tabs)	bd ⎫ for 28 days
		5 ml (1 tab)	qds ⎭
Benzylpenicillin	IV	300–600 mg (0.5–1.0 Mu)	qds
Bricanyl	See terbutaline		
Brufen	See ibuprofen		
Buprenorphine	SL	200–400 µg	6–8 hourly
Buscopan	See hyoscine butylbromide		

Table 2.32 (*continued*)

Drug	Route	Dose	Frequency
Canesten	See clotrimazole		
Capoten			
Capozide	See under Oral drugs — ACE inhibitors		
Captopril			
Carace	See lisinopril		
Carbamazepine	po	200 mg	bd. Max 600 mg bd
Cefotaxime	IV	1 g	tds
Cefuroxime	IV	750 mg	tds
Ceftazidime	IV	1 g	tds
Cephalexin	po	500 mg	tds
Chloramphenicol	Topical eye treatment, 1 drop 3 hourly		
Chlormethiazole	See under Oral drugs and Drug infusions		
Chlorpromazine	See under The confused patient (Chapter 6)		
Cimetidine	po	400 mg	bd
		800 mg	nocte
	IV	200 mg	qds
Ciprofloxacin	po	500 mg	bd
	IV	100–200 mg	bd over 30–60 min
Cisapride	po	10 mg	tds/qds
Clotrimazole	Topical cream, apply to affected area bd/tds		
	Vaginal tablets, insert one 500 mg tablet at night, once		
Co-codamol	po	1–2 tabs	4 hourly. Max 8/day
Codeine phosphate	po/IM	30–60 mg	4 hourly. Max 180 mg/day
Co-dydramol	po	1–2 tabs	4 hourly. Max 8/day
Colofac	See mebeverine hydrochloride		
Colven	po	1 sachet	bd; 30 min pre-meal
Co-proxamol	po	1–2 tabs	4 hourly. Max 8/day
Cordarone	See under Amiodarone		
DeNol	See bismuth chelate		
Diclofenac	po	25–50 mg	bd/tds
	IM	75 mg	bd; max 2 days
Diamorphine	SC or IM	5–10 mg	4 hourly

Table 2.32 (*continued*)

Drug	Route	Dose	Frequency
Diazepam	po	2–5 mg	tds
Diltiazem	po	60 mg	tds; max 480 mg/day
DF 118	See dihydrocodeine		
Digoxin	See under Oral drugs		
Dihydrocodeine	po	30 mg	4 hourly
	IM/SC	50 mg	4–6 hourly
Dobutamine	See under Drug infusions		
Dopamine	See under Drug infusions		
Doxapram	See under Drug infusions		
Enalapril	po	Initially 2.5 mg Increase to 10–20 mg if tolerated	Maintenance: max 40 mg/day for hypertension
Epanutin	See phenytoin		
Epilim	See sodium valproate		
Erythromycin	po/IV	500 mg	qds
	See Table 2.2(b) for IV administration		
Ferrous sulphate	po	200 mg	bd/tds
Flucloxacillin	po/IV	500 mg	qds
Frumil	po	1–2 tabs	mane
Frusemide	po/IV	40 mg	od but doses can vary enormously
Fusidic acid	po/IV	500 mg	tds
Fybogel	See ispaghula husk		
Gastrocote	po	1–2 tabs chewed	qds after meals and at bedtime
		5–15 ml	qds after meals and at bedtime
Gaviscon	po	1–2 tabs chewed qds or 10–20 ml after meals and at bedtime, followed by water	
Gentamicin	See under Gentamicin nomogram		
Glibenclamide	po	5 mg increased to 15 mg od as necessary	
Glycerin suppositories	prn	1	prn
Glyceryl trinitrate	SL	1–2 tabs	prn
	Buccal spray	1–2 puffs	prn

Table 2.32 *(continued)*

Drug	Route	Dose	Frequency
Haloperidol	See under The confused patient (Chapter 6)		
Heminevrin	See chlormethiazole		
Heparin	See under Drug infusions		
Hydrocortisone (for acute asthma)	IV	200 mg stat then 100 mg qds for 24 h	
Hyoscine butylbromide	po/IM	20 mg	qds
Ibuprofen	po	400 mg	tds
Imodium	See under Diarrhoea (Chapter 6)		
Indomethacin	po	25–50 mg	tds
Insulins	See under Drug infusions and the *British National Formulary*		
Ipratropium bromide	Inhaler	2 puffs	qds
	Nebuliser	250–500 µg	bd/qds
Isoprenaline	See under Drug infusions		
Isosorbide mononitrate	po	10–20 mg	bd
Isosorbide dinitrate	po	10–40 mg	tds
	IV	See under Drug infusions — Nitrates	
Ispaghula husk	po	1 sachet	bd
Lactulose	po	10–20 ml	bd
Largactil	See chlorpromazine		
Lasix	See frusemide		
Lisinopril	po	Initially 2.5 mg, increasing to 10–20 mg/day	
Lofepramine	po	70 mg	bd/tds
Lomotil	po	4 tabs stat, then 2 tabs 6 hourly till diarrhoea is controlled	
Loperamide	See under Diarrhoea (Chapter 6)		
Losec	See omeprazole		
Magnesium trisilicate	po	10 ml	tds
Maxolon	See metoclopramide		
Mebeverine hydrochloride	po	1 tab	tds, 20 min pre-meal
Metformin	po	500 mg 850 mg	tds, or bd. Max 3 g/day in divided doses
Methyldopa	po	250 mg	bd/tds; max 3 g/day
Metoclopramide	po/IM/IV	10 mg	8 hourly
Metolazone	po	5–10 mg mane	Increase to max 80 mg daily

Table 2.32 (*continued*)

Drug	Route	Dose	Frequency
Metronidazole	po	400 mg	tds
	IV/pr	500 mg	tds
Milpar	po	10–20 ml	bd
Misoprostol			
1 Treatment of ulcers	po	800 μg	2–4 divided doses for 4 weeks
2 Prophylaxis	po	200 μg	bd/qds
Morphine	SC/IM	10 mg	4 hourly
Naloxone	IV	For the emergency treatment of opiate poisoning: 0.4–2.0 mg repeated at intervals of 2–3 min. Max dose 10 mg	
Naproxen	po	250 –500 mg	bd
Nifedipine SR	po	10–20 mg	bd
Nystatin	For oral thrush, topical 100 000 u qds after food		
Omeprazole	po	20 mg	od; 4 weeks for duodenal ulcers; 8 weeks for gastric ulcers. 40 mg bd for oesophagitis
Omnopon	See papaveretum		
Omnopon and aspirin	po	1–2 tabs	4–6 hourly; max 8/day
Oxygen	See under Oxygen administration		
Papaveretum	IM	10–20 mg	4 hourly
Paracetamol	po	1000 mg	4 hourly; max 4 g/day
Penicillin V	See phenoxymethylpenicillin		
Pethidine	po	50–150 mg	4 hourly
	IM	25–100 mg	4 hourly
Phenoxymethylpenicillin	po	250–500 mg	qds
Phenytoin	po	Initially 150–300 mg daily, increased gradually as necessary. Max 600 mg od	
	IV	See under Drug infusions	
Phosphate enema	pr	1	od/PRN
Potassium	po/IV	See under Drug infusions	
Prednisolone	See under Oral drugs		
Prepulsid	See cisapride		

Table 2.32 *(continued)*

Drug	Route	Dose	Frequency
Pro-Banthine	See propantheline bromide		
Prochlorperazine	IM	12.5 mg	6 hourly
	po	5 mg	8 hourly
Propantheline bromide	po	15 mg	tds at least 1 h pre-meal plus 30 mg nocte
Quinine sulphate for night cramps	po	200–300 mg	nocte
Ranitidine	po	150 mg	bd
		300 mg	nocte
	IV	50 mg	tds; dilute in at least 20 ml water
Regulan	See ispaghula husk		
Salbutamol	po	4 mg	tds/qds
	Inhaler	1–2 puffs	bd/qds
	Nebuliser	2.5–5.0 mg	qds
	Infusion	See under Drug infusions	
Senna	po	2 tabs	bd
Sodium valproate	po	200 mg initially tds, increasing by 200 mg/day at 3 day intervals to max 2.5 g daily	
Stemetil	See prochlorperazine		
Streptokinase	See under Drug infusions — Thrombolytic therapy		
Tagamet	See cimetidine		
Temazepam	See under Oral drugs		
Temgesic	See buprenorphine		
Tenormin	See atenolol		
Terbutaline	Inhaler	1–2 puffs	bd/qds
	Nebuliser	5–10 mg	bd/qds
	IV (see under Drug infusions)		
Tetracycline	po	250–500 mg	qds
Theophylline	See individual drugs in the *British National Formulary* and see under Drug infusions		
Trimethoprim	po	200 mg	bd
Vasopressin	See under Drug infusions		
Ventolin	See salbutamol		
Voltarol	See diclofenac		
Warfarin	See under Oral anticoagulation therapy		
Zantac	See ranitidine		
Zestril	See lisinopril		

3: Practical Procedures

This chapter deals with the manner of performing several procedures that most house officers will find themselves involved with. It is purposefully basic in its approach. Even when you have mastered the techniques we hope that you will continue to find the apparatus lists helpful in preparing for a procedure. If you need to know about more complex procedures we recommend you read an excellent book, *Procedures in Practice* (1988) British Medical Journal, London, or read the relevant sections in Sprigings, D. and Chambers, J. (1990) *Acute Medicine*, Blackwell Scientific Publications, Oxford.

Arterial blood gas estimation

APPARATUS
1 Cotton wool ball.
2 Either use a prepared blood gas syringe or make your own as follows.
   (a) Take a 2 ml syringe with a 239 needle or 21 G butterfly.
   (b) Take up any strength of heparin (1000, 5000 or 25 000 u) into this syringe and needle.
   (c) Expose all of the syringe to heparin by withdrawing plunger to full extent and rotating heparin around barrel.
   (d) Expel heparin.

SITE
Either the radial or the femoral artery. (The brachial artery is not to be recommended because it is a small-end artery.) If using the radial artery it is wise to check for the presence of a patent ulnar artery — apply pressure over both the ulnar and

radial artery at the wrist so as to prevent blood flow. Ask the patient to open and close their fist 15 times. Release pressure on the ulnar artery and check that the fingers flush red indicating a patent ulnar artery. Remember that the femoral nerve lies lateral to the femoral artery — thus err on the side of caution; approach the artery towards its medial side.

PROCEDURE
Very dependent on practice. Useful points:

1 Make sure that the part of the patient to be used is on a stable surface and the patient is comfortable.

2 Take time to palpate the position of the artery with index and middle finger of one hand, holding the syringe in the other.

3 Approach radial artery at 45°: femoral artery at 90° (Fig. 3.1(a)).

4 If not successful on first entry, withdraw until needle is almost out of the skin.

5 Relocate artery with free fingers.

6 Advance and withdraw in an ordered fashion (Fig. 3.1(b)) until blood suddenly enters syringe. Ready prepared syringes will normally fill automatically, self-prepared syringes may require assistance — use your free fingers to pull back gently on the plunger.

7 Withdraw and apply firm pressure to the puncture site for at least 5 min.

8 Make sure there are no air bubbles within the blood sample, remove the needle and cap the sample.

9 Transfer sample to an analyser within 5–10 min preferably on ice.

10 Note the oxygen concentration of inspired gas and write this and the results in the notes.

11 Avoid checking blood gas levels within 20 min of a change in the inspired oxygen concentration because the arterial oxygen concentration will not have had time to equilibrate.

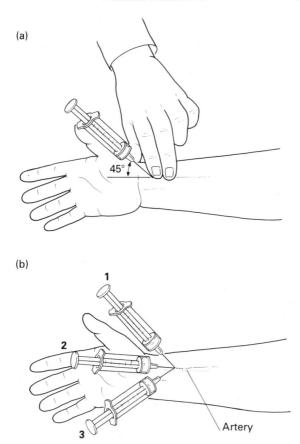

Fig. 3.1. Arterial blood gas sampling.

NB: Many doctors like to infiltrate the skin over the chosen artery with 1% lignocaine. Opinion varies as to whether this is necessary. Be guided by the attitude of your patient to blood tests. If you have had problems in the past obtaining an arterial sample from a particular patient, use local anaesthetic on future occasions with that patient.

INTERPRETATION OF RESULTS (Table 3.1)

Table 3.1 Understanding blood gas results — hydrogen ion homeostasis

	pH	P_{CO_2}	HCO_3	Potassium level
(a) Acidosis				
1 Metabolic				
Initial state	↓	N	↓	usually ↑
Compensated	N	↓	↓	(↓ in renal tubular acidosis)
2 Respiratory				
Acute change	↓	↑	N or ↑	↑
Compensated	N	↑	↑↑	
(b) Alkalosis				
1 Metabolic				
Acute state	↑	N	↑	↓
Chronic state	↑	N or ↑	↑↑	
2 Respiratory				
Acute state	↑	↓	N or ↓	↓
Compensated	N	↓	↓↓	

Straight (underlined) arrows show primary change.
Arrows in italic type show compensatory change.
Reproduced from Zilva, J.F., Pannall, P.R. & Mayne, P. (1989) *Clinical Chemistry in Diagnosis and Treatment* with permission of Hodder & Stoughton Limited, London.

Normal values

pH	7.35–7.45
$P_{a}CO_2$	4.5–6.0 kPa (35–45 mmHg)
Base excess	± 2 mmol/l
$P_{a}O_2$	10–14 kPa (90–105 mmHg)
plasma HCO_3	22–26 mmol/l
O_2 saturation	95–100%
Type 1 respiratory failure:	$P_{a}O_2$ less than 8.0 (less than 60 mmol/l)
	$P_{a}CO_2$ less than 6.0 kPa (less than 45 mmHg)
Type 2 respiratory failure:	$P_{a}O_2$ less than 8.0 (less than 60 mmol/l)
	$P_{a}CO_2$ greater than 6.0 kPa (greater than 45 mmHg)

NB: Very poor blood gas results may indicate that you have obtained a venous sample. This can be easily verified by the percentage saturation result. Over 80% saturation suggests arterial blood, whereas 50% or less saturation suggests venous blood.

Bladder catheterisation

You will normally only be asked to catheterise male patients but unfortunately if the nursing staff are unable to catheterise a female patient despite all their years of experience *you* will be asked to attempt it — and it may be your first time. Good luck! If possible ask somebody more experienced than yourself to oversee your attempts.

Males

APPARATUS
1 Catheterisation pack — kidney bowl, gauze swabs, sterile towels, gallipot etc.
2 Sterile gloves.
3 Lignocaine gel.
4 Cleaning solution.
5 Foley catheter: 14 G is a good size to start with for an uncomplicated case. (A size 12 is smaller than a size 14).
6 5–10 ml syringe containing 5–10 ml sterile water to inflate balloon.
7 Urine bag.
8 Bag stand.

PROCEDURE
1 Open up the catheter pack and then remove the outer non-sterile covers from items **2**, **3**, **4** and **5** in the list above, placing the contents onto the sterile surface.
2 Having washed your hands, put on gloves and cover genital area with sterile towels leaving only the penis exposed. Open

the lignocaine gel pack and screw the nozzle onto the tube whilst both hands are sterile. Retract the foreskin and clean the urethral opening with cleaning solution. Keep one hand clean throughout — this should be the hand you will use to insert the catheter.

3 Introduce lignocaine gel via a nozzle into the urethral opening — squeeze in the whole tube and then pause momentarily.

4 Open catheter wrapping at tip end only and insert into penis until fully in, withdrawing plastic covering in stages; this is often very difficult and the whole procedure can rapidly become unsterile but try pulling the wrapping off from the distal end by shaking it from side to side to allow the catheter to fall out.

If any difficulty is found with insertion, try elevating the shaft of the penis so as to straighten the urethra. Alternatively in some patients you will find success by pulling the shaft of the penis down between the patient's thighs. *Never* use force.

5 Once fully in, inflate the balloon by injecting 5–10 ml of water into the one-way valve. If this produces pain *stop* because you may still be in the urethra.

Note: some new catheters have a ready filled bag of water at one end from which you need to release the clamp by twisting with force. Squeezing the bag will inflate the balloon in the distal end of the catheter.

6 If urine fails to flow immediately it may be because the catheter is blocked with gel. Aspirate the catheter free end with a 10 ml syringe to clear gel or apply gentle pressure above the pubic symphysis to encourage urine flow.

7 *Put back the foreskin.*

8 Send a catheter specimen of urine for culture.

PROBLEMS

If you fail to catheterise successfully:

• Try a smaller size.

• Try a 'silastic' catheter which is a little firmer. You could also cool the catheter to harden it.

- Ask a senior member of your team.
- Refer the patient to the surgeons for insertion of a suprapubic catheter. If urine by-passes the catheter, flush or replace it with a *smaller* size.

Females

APPARATUS
As for males.

PROCEDURE
1 Follow step **1** as for males.
2 Don gloves and ask patient to lie flat on the bed, bend her knees and, with her ankles resting together, to let her legs flop into full abduction (i.e. the same position as is used for a vaginal examination).
3 Place sterile towels and separate the labia minora with your left thumb and index finger and clean the area with cleaning solution.
4 Isolate the external urethral meatus just posterior to the clitoris and introduce lubricated tip of catheter into urethra. As the female urethra is relatively short and straight, catheterisation is rarely a problem.

Blood cultures

APPARATUS
1 Pair of blood culture bottles.
2 Cotton-wool ball.
3 Alcohol wipes.
4 2 × 21 G needles.
5 20 ml syringe.

PROCEDURE
1 Swab area with three alcohol wipes and allow to dry.
2 *Do not* relocate the vein with your fingers unless wearing sterile gloves.

3 Withdraw 20 ml of blood.

4 Use a fresh, sterile needle to inject 6 ml of blood into each bottle, having swabbed the top of the bottle with an alcohol wipe.

NB: Changing the needle between bottles has now been shown to be unnecessary.

5 Place into an incubator as soon as possible.

Central lines and CVP measurement

Depending on the speciality of your job and your luck, you may be presented with the opportunity of inserting a central line. This is a technically difficult and intricate procedure and is best learnt with expert supervision and repetitive demonstrations. We have not described this procedure here because there are many varying methods and it is better that you are shown the procedure by somebody skilled at it. We have included an apparatus list to help you set things up for when you do eventually do one.

APPARATUS

1 Central line: 14 G is bigger than 17 G. 17 G is suitable for most indications.

2 Sterile gloves.

3 Iodine skin sterilising solution.

4 Suture and needle (e.g. 2/0 nylon).

5 Sterile pack containing gallipot, towels and gauze swabs.

6 Lignocaine 2%.

7 Needles (orange — 25 G and green — 21 G) and syringes (5 ml, 10 ml).

Don't forget

Having inserted the line you must check its position with a CXR. If the line is in the superior vena cava then the fluid level in the CVP tubing should rise and fall a few millimetres with respiration. If it does not then either:

1 It is outside the vein or only partially in, or the tip may be angled against the vein wall. Adjust position under sterile conditions.

2 The catheter is partially blocked — see below.

3 The catheter is in the right ventricle — withdraw slightly under sterile conditions.

PROBLEMS

Once inserted, there are potential complications that you will be called upon to manage:

Sepsis

If a patient with a central line *in situ* develops a temperature, take blood cultures via the line *as well as* from the peripheral veins. If the patient is septic the line should be removed as it may represent the source of infection.

NB: Whenever removing a central line, the tip should be cut off with a sterile blade, labelled and sent to microbiology for culture and sensitivity studies.

Blockage

It is important to maintain a continuous flow through the line or to flush it at least daily with heparinised saline to prevent clotting. If a blockage does occur it may be possible to remove it by aspirating the line with a 50 ml syringe. If this doesn't work, try flushing the line with 5 ml of heparinised saline via a 5 ml syringe at moderate pressure.

Measurement of CVP

This plays an important role in the management of many conditions. The central line is connected by way of a three-way tap to a water manometer. The scale on the manometer is positioned with a spirit level so that the **'10 cm' mark** is level with a fixed reference point on the patient — hence the patient should always be in the same position when measurements are taken. This fixed reference point is either: (a) the midpoint of the axilla; or (b) the sternomanubrial joint.

Always adjust the level of the scale so that the 10 cm mark is *exactly* level with the reference point. The use of the 10 cm mark rather than the zero allows for 'negative' readings to be measured.

TO TAKE A READING
1 Lie the patient in the standard position.
2 Check that the 10 cm mark on the manometer is still level with the reference point.
3 Close the three-way tap to the patient.
4 Run 20 ml of fluid into the manometer from the reservoir fluid bag.
5 Close the manometer to the reservoir.
6 Rotate the tap so that the line is open between the patient and manometer. The manometer fluid level should swing with respiration and settle to the appropriate level. The CVP is then measured in centimetres of water.

Normal range for a horizontally lying patient
If the '10 cm' mark is level with the midpoint of the axilla, normal range = 11–18 cm.
If the '10 cm' mark is level with the sternomanubrial joint, normal range = 6–14 cm.
NB: If the reference point is placed level with the **'0' cm mark** on the manometer scale, the normal values will be 10 cm lower for each of the figures given above.

Measurements are affected by pressure within the superior vena cava which is in turn affected by right atrial pressure. Right atrial pressure is affected by:
1 Intrathoracic pressure — the CVP level thus fluctuates with respiration.

2 The volume of the intravascular compartment — thus serial CVP measurements can be useful in monitoring blood replacement.

3 Venous tone — thus any cause of raised catecholamine levels (e.g. haemorrhagic shock or dobutamine infusion) will raise the CVP. Because of this, a patient may lose a significant amount of blood but still maintain a stable CVP. Particular care must be taken in the elderly, whose compensatory mechanisms in the face of volume overload or depletion are often unpredictable.

4 Right ventricular function — this is impaired in acute right heart failure (e.g. acute PE or large MI). Absolute CVP measurements may be meaningless in these situations and a Swan–Ganz catheter used indirectly to measure left atrial pressure may be more useful. Serial CVP measurements however can still be useful.

NB: If called about dramatic changes in the CVP level check the result yourself.

If the result has changed dramatically, look for a cause (Table 3.2) and treat appropriately. If the CVP drops due to hypovolaemia replace fluids with colloid initially (e.g. Haemaccel 1 u half-hourly) or blood (if you suspect a bleed or the haemoglobin is below 10 g/dl) — see under Gastrointestinal bleeding and Hypotension (Chapter 6).

OTHER USES OF CENTRAL LINES

1 Rapid infusion of fluid.

2 Multiple infusions.

3 To withdraw blood — provided the first 20 ml is discarded and a sterile technique is used.

4 To give substances which are irritant or dangerous unless dissolved by rapid blood flow, e.g. total parenteral nutrition.

Table 3.2 Causes of an alteration in the CVP

If the CVP rises think of:
1 Incorrect measurement — check that the reference point is level with the chosen point on the manometer scale.
2 Congestive cardiac failure.
3 Pulmonary embolism.
4 Tension pneumothorax.
5 Fluid overload.
6 Right ventricular failure.
7 Cardiac tamponade.

If the CVP drops think of:
1 Incorrect measurement — check that the reference point is level with the chosen point on the manometer scale.
2 Hypovolaemia.
3 Sepsis.
4 Drugs/poisoning.
5 Left ventricular failure.

Chest drains

These may be inserted for the treatment of a pneumothorax or for the removal of large quantities of pleural fluid. As with central lines we do not attempt to describe the insertion of chest drains because the procedure is intricate and requires repeated demonstration. However, once a drain has been inserted you will be required to manage the patient and any ensuing problems.

Remember that chest drains hurt. Ensure the patient has access to adequate analgesia if required. Some doctors prefer to inject bupivacaine (Marcain) around the drain site.

Note

1 You should *never* clamp a 'swinging' chest drain; clamping leads to collapse of the lung. If the patient is being moved then be extremely careful that the 'underwater seal' does *not* tip over.

2 If the fluid level in the underwater seal stops swinging with respiration, there may be a blockage in the tubing which can be removed by 'milking the line' with a pair of 'milkers' — ask somebody to show you how to do this.

DECIDING WHEN TO REMOVE A DRAIN

This should probably not be your decision.

1 Pneumothorax: wait until air fails to bubble in the bottle when the patient inspires deeply or coughs (usually 48 h), then obtain a CXR. If this reveals a significant amount of air in the pleural space then leave well alone for a further 24 h and repeat the CXR. If the pneumothorax has resolved, clamp the tubing (using two clamps) and obtain another CXR 24 h later. If at this stage there is no significant pneumothorax, withdraw the drain (see below).

2 Drainage of large pleural effusions: drainage may continue for several days at a rate of no more than 4 litres/day and no more than 1.5 litres in any 1 h period because this can cause mediastinal shift and resultant asphyxia or pulmonary oedema. Remove the drain when the effusion is shown to have completely drained on a CXR. You may want to consider a chemical pleurodesis; discuss this with your team.

REMOVAL OF A CHEST DRAIN

You have spent several days removing air or fluid from the patient's pleural cavity. Unfortunately you can reverse all of the effort by withdrawing the drain incorrectly.

Before commencing, give some analgesia — IM opiates if necessary. The basic point to remember is that as you remove the drain it is essential to have a positive intrathoracic pressure. This may be achieved by asking the patient to perform the Valsalva manoeuvre. Everybody knows how to do this but they don't know that that's what it's called! It is most effectively described as 'what you do when straining on the toilet' or 'what you did to make the blood rush to your face as a child'. Demonstrate the effect to the patient — carefully! Explain that you will require him/her to perform this forced expiration for at least 30 s. Once you are happy that the patient will be able to maintain the correct intrathoracic pressure, proceed as follows:

1 Ask somebody to help you. One of you will be responsible for removing the drain whilst the other person pulls the closing suture together to close the hole to the pleura. (This closing suture is often called a 'purse string' suture.)

2 Put on sterile gloves.

3 Remove dressing from around the drain.

4 Cut the suture which is restraining the drain (make sure that you are not cutting the closing suture!).

5 Ask the patient to take a deep breath in and then to carry out the Valsalva manoevre. (They must be at full inspiration.)

6 Withdraw the drain. As you do so you may hear a reassuring rush of air as the last intrapleural gas is expelled, confirming that the patient has co-operated correctly. As the last bit of the drain is withdrawn pull the closing suture firmly but gently together.

7 Apply a light sterile dressing to the puncture site (with a blob of collodion on to plug the hole).

8 Obtain a further CXR.

ECGs

This section is not intended to help you with the interpretation of an ECG. For guidance on this subject you are referred to the many books on the subject such as Hampton, J. R. (1986) *The ECG Made Easy* Churchill Livingstone, Edinburgh. Our aim here is to give you practical advice on performing ECGs and problems you may encounter.

Whenever you have to perform an ECG, make sure you have all the necessary equipment. There is nothing more annoying than picking up an ECG machine from another ward, getting to the patient and realising that you have left half of the equipment behind.

If it is the patient's first ECG, be sure to reassure them that you are not connecting them to the national electricity grid! Attach the limb leads to hairless areas of the inner forearm just above the wrist and the outer aspects of the leg above the ankle. The wires are normally labelled but if not they usually attach as follows:

Right arm: Red
Left arm: Yellow
Left leg: Green
Right leg: Black

Avoid bony points. Use electrode jelly (KY or Clinijel will suffice) or more conveniently alcohol wipes at each attachment site. If there is a screw attaching the wires to the electrodes, ensure this is tight. The electrode from the right leg is only to earth the patient and has no bearing on the recording.

For chest leads, be careful not to overlap the jelly areas or spurious results may be obtained. These can resemble acute ischaemia which is obviously very important clinically. Localised shaving may be necessary to assist attachment but if the worst comes to the worst, hold the electrode in place through a gloved hand.

Chest lead attachment (Fig. 3.2)

V1: Fourth intercostal space, right of the sternum.
V2: Fourth intercostal space, left of the sternum.
V3: Between V2 and V4.
V4: Left 5th intercostal space in the mid-clavicular line.
V5: Anterior axillary line level with V4.
V6: Mid-axillary line, level with V4.

HINTS

1 If the patient has a tremor of the hand an electrode on the upper arm may yield a better record.
2 You can attach an electrode to an amputation stump but if it is very short there is no problem placing two leads on the

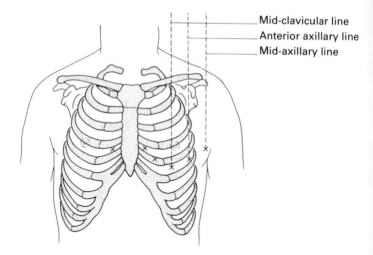

Fig. 3.2 The positions of the conventional chest leads. Note that the first intercostal space is immediately above and the second intercostal space is immediately below the sternal angle.

opposite leg. Crossing the leg leads does not matter but if the arm leads are reversed the limb lead recordings will be inverted.

3 Make sure that the leads to the patient do not run parallel to a mains lead, e.g. one running to a ripple bed.

4 The patient should be lying down unsupported by any muscular effort and relaxed. S/he should be warm and should keep still and silent and preferably hold his or her breath during the recording.

Exercise stress tests

Your first few stress tests will probably stress you more than the patient! The results are difficult to analyse unless you push the patient and you often have to persuade the patient to continue longer than they would otherwise want to. Take comfort in the fact that most cardiac technicians are excellent at what they do and, if you're lucky, will guide you slowly through your initial tests. You should ask somebody to show you the routine and give you advice on when to stop before you have to take charge yourself. The major purposes of the test are:

1 Detection of coronary artery disease.
2 Assessment of severity.
3 Precipitation of arrhythmias.

Contra-indications

Some are only relative contra-indications and you should check with your seniors in all of these cases whether you should proceed.

- Uncontrolled arrhythmias.
- Severe aortic stenosis (gradient greater than 50 mmHg with a normal left ventricle).
- Systolic BP greater than 200 mmHg, and diastolic BP greater than 100 mmHg.
- Unstable angina.
- Left bundle branch block on ECG — because it is difficult to interpret — but may be useful to assess exercise tolerance.
- Hypertrophic obstructive cardiomyopathy.

PROCEDURE

1 Ensure that you have adequate resuscitation equipment available; cardiac arrest occurs in approximately 1 in 4000 exercise tests. A doctor must be present at all times during the test especially during the recovery period when VT is most likely to occur.
2 Consider which protocol you are going to use; either Bruce or Modified Bruce. Check with your seniors.
3 Calculate the predicted peak heart rate (= 220 minus the age of the patient). Note that beta-blockers should be stopped 2 days before the test.
4 Do a resting ECG and check this before beginning.

5 Check the resting BP.

6 During the test you will be required to keep an eye on the monitor for ST depression/elevation and frequency of ectopics, and to perform regular BP checks. This may be difficult because the arm will be moving around — if you have problems, at least palpate the systolic BP.

If you're lucky, most of the test protocol is performed automatically and your main decision will be when to stop. Cease the test if the patient has:

- progressive severe chest pain
- a fall in systolic BP of more than 20 mmHg
- severe progressive symptoms: faintness/dizziness — especially if pale and clammy; dyspnoea; exhaustion
- progressive ST elevation — if it is associated with chest pain it may indicate a critical lesion — administer GTN
- ST depression greater than or equal to 2 mm (horizontal or down sloping)
- three or more consecutive ventricular ectopics.
- a fall in heart rate
- ventricular tachycardia or ventricular fibrillation!
- attained peak heart rate.

7 Continue to monitor the patient with BP and pulse checks at regular intervals until the BP and pulse have returned to pre-stress levels — a significant number of tests become positive during the recovery phase and there are often ventricular ectopics at this stage.

Feeding

It is worthwhile remembering that patients receiving IV fluids are being given very few calories (e.g. 1 litre of 5% dextrose contains only 200 kcal). An optimal nutritional state is essential for improvement in health, so involve the dietitian early in the management of all your patients. Consider nasogastric or parenteral feeding sooner rather than later.

Total parenteral nutrition

Patients receiving total parenteral nutrition require close monitoring — generally by you! The following is information regarding the management of such patients. The individual details will vary from place to place.

Central venous catheters

A central venous catheter used for parenteral feeding should not be used for administering drugs or blood products, withdrawing blood samples or for the measurement of CVP. Central venous catheters previously inserted for drug administration or CVP measurement must not be used for parenteral nutrition. You can, however, take blood from 'triple lumen' lines.

MONITORING PATIENTS RECEIVING TOTAL PARENTERAL NUTRITION

Clinical monitoring

Temperature and pulse	4 hourly
Blood glucose (BM Stix)	6 hourly initially then as required after the first 48 h
Fluid balance	Daily
Skinfold thickness	Twice weekly
Mid-arm circumference	Twice weekly
Handgrip dynamometry	Twice weekly
Weight	Twice weekly

Assess patient for signs of fluid overload at least twice daily — listen to the chest, check for swelling of ankles and check fluid balance.

Laboratory monitoring

Daily	Full blood count, U & E, blood glucose, 24 h urine collection for urinalysis
Twice weekly	Calcium and phosphate, albumin, LFTs
Weekly	Coagulation studies and assay of trace elements (e.g. magnesium and zinc)

Take a sample for baseline vitamin B_{12}, serum and red cell folate, zinc and copper estimation.

Nasogastric feeding (enteral feeding)

Enteral feeding via a nasogastric feeding tube requires less monitoring compared with total parenteral nutrition because the GI tract's natural regulatory mechanisms are still intact. However in many hospitals more responsibility may fall on your shoulders in terms of deciding which feeding regimen to employ. If you're lucky, your hospital dietitian will be able to advise you on which feeds to prescribe. They should undertake a thorough assessment of the patient's nutritional status in order to decide on the type of feed required.

The choice is complex because there are now an enormous number of types of feed available, some of which contain whole protein and other large molecules, and others which are termed 'elemental' because they contain amino acids, oligosaccharides, monosaccharides and short chain fatty acids. Some feeds contain a standard amount of calories and protein whereas others may contain a low or high concentration of these constituents. The choice will depend on the patient's general condition, weight and state of nutrition. Almost all have 1 kcal/ml except a few with 1.5 kcal/ml, which are always identified by name (e.g. Ensure Plus).

The feeds are administered by way of a pump or by employing gravity and generally the administration is continued for long periods of time, e.g. 12–24 h. If you are to start enteral feeding for a patient who has been able to take even small amounts of food, you can usually begin with a full strength, isotonic feed. However if the gut has been previously rested you may need to introduce the feed slowly. Ask for advice. As a general guide give 20–50 ml water/h for 6 h. Aspirate at this point and if there is little or no aspirate then introduce half-strength feed at a rate of 30–60 ml/h for a further 6–12 h. Aspirate 3 hourly and if there continues to be little or no aspirate, continue to strengthen the feed up to full strength.

Much of the day-to-day management of this feeding regimen will be up to the nursing staff and they should be aware of how often to aspirate the tube. One point to note is the need to aspirate the tube at night even if the feeding regimen is well established because the flat lying position can impair gastric emptying. Beware of the effect of metoclopramide in speeding gastric transition and the effect of opiates in slowing it down.

Diarrhoea is a common problem and may result from lactose intolerance, infected feeds, or too rapid introduction. Look for other possible causes such as antibiotics; if none is found, treat symptomatically. If the patient experiences pain, slow down the infusion.

Hickman lines

These are essentially central lines except that the point of skin entry is further away from the vein than usual, because the line is tunnelled under the skin. This is thought to reduce the chance of infection.

These lines are commonly used in patients receiving long-term cytotoxics who are neutropenic and thus prone to infection: they must therefore be handled with great care and with strong emphasis on a sterile technique. Many nurses have not been formally trained to handle Hickman lines. You will find yourself being asked not only to connect various infusions but also to disconnect them: they can therefore become very labour-intensive for you. (This is a ridiculous situation given that nurses are infinitely better at aseptic procedures than doctors!) Below is a description of a suitable way of using these lines. We have chosen the setting up of a 40 ml daunorubicin infusion as an example.

SETTING UP AN INFUSION VIA A HICKMAN LINE

1 Ask someone to help you because it is always easier to

maintain sterility if there are two of you.

2 Collect together the apparatus needed:
- infusion pump
- one-litre bag of 0.9% sodium chloride
- ampoule of anti-emetic
- giving set
- syringe of cytotoxic — check name, date, dosage and time drug was made up
- 10 ml heparinised saline
- 3 × 21 G needles and 1 × 16 G needle
- sterile gloves
- alcohol wipes
- 3 × 5 ml syringes
- sterile bung.

3 Put on gown and sterile gloves.

4 Ask helper to attach giving set to infusion bag without touching the end of the line or the rubber connector.

5 Ask for any non-sterile objects to be opened up for you.

6 Shut gate/clamp on Hickman line (if not already shut).

7 Using alcohol wipes to avoid glove contact with the line, take end bung off the Hickman line and discard.

8 Flush line with 5 ml heparinised saline, opening and closing the gate as appropriate.

9 Inject the anti-emetic — again opening and shutting the gate.

10 Connect the saline drip and infuse slowly.

11 You can then 'piggy-back' the daunorubicin into the line already established by cleaning the rubber end of the giving set, introducing the white needle (connected to the syringe of cytotoxic) into the rubber, and infusing over about 10–20 min.

12 Once the cytotoxic drug is finished, continue saline for a minute or two before flushing with heparinised saline.

13 Finally, re-bung the Hickman line and close the gate.

Hints
- Touch the Hickman line as little as possible.
- Always open and shut the gate between procedures.
- Teach the patient to look after his/her line.

You can take blood from a Hickman line if absolutely necessary, as long as you discard the first 20 ml; Hickman line blood is not suitable for gentamicin levels because aminoglycosides are adsorbed onto the line.

If you are to set up a blood transfusion, set up a small bag of 0.9% sodium chloride and run it in very slowly whilst the nursing staff wait for the blood to arrive. They can then connect the bag of blood to the line already *in situ* and should not have to call you back — hopefully.

Injections

You will infrequently be required to perform SC or IM injections. Try to perfect a painless technique.

Subcutaneous

1 After explaining what you are about to do, assist the patient into a suitable position.
2 Use the smallest possible needle, swab the area to be used and grasp the skin between forefinger and thumb.
3 Let the needle rest on the skin for 3–5 s before pushing in at 45°. (The idea is to separate the stimuli of touch and pain so that the patient, being occupied with touch, is less sensitive to pain.)
4 Release the skin, pull back the plunger and if no blood is aspirated, depress the plunger and inject slowly. If you do aspirate blood, withdraw the needle, replace it and start again. Explain to the patient that you have had to use another injection site because it is unsafe to inject directly into the vein.
5 Remember to sign for the drug.

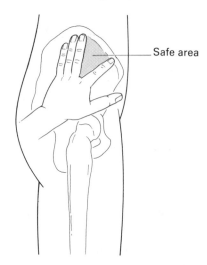

Safe area

Fig. 3.3 Where to give IM injections.

Intramuscular

The deltoid muscle will accommodate small injections but for
larger ones the buttock is best. The 'upper and outer' quadrant
as near to the iliac crest as possible is advised, to avoid damage
to the sciatic nerve (Fig. 3.3). If you draw an imaginary line
between the greater trochanter of the femur and the anterior
superior iliac spine and inject above that line, you will be
injecting away from the nerve.

It is useful to pull the skin and SC tissues taut before
introducing the needle at 90° so that these tissues break the
needle track when they fall back. Remember, always, to
aspirate before injecting to make sure you are not in a blood
vessel — see above.

Inhaler techniques

Salbutamol, ipratropium and beclomethasone are often prescribed in the inhaler form. Patients are frequently found to

have a less than optimal technique and maximum therapeutic benefit may not be obtained. If you have a patients on this form of medication ensure that they use it effectively — if you don't, nobody else will.

CORRECT TECHNIQUE

1 Shake container.

2 Exhale fully.

3 Place mouthpiece into mouth.

4 As you begin to inhale deeply, press the plunger of the inhaler down.

5 Count to at least 'ten' before breathing out.

6 Repeat as per prescription.

If using a beta-agonist such as salbutamol and an inhaled steroid, use the bronchodilating beta-agonist 10 min before the steroid to maximise penetration of the latter.

Point **4** above is the part that presents the most problems but it is the most important part of the procedure. Thus it should be practised over and over again until perfected: try to get hold of a practice inhaler for this purpose. If the patient is completely unable to cope with the sequence of events for whatever reason, you could consider using a 'spacer' device, which reduces the need for perfect co-ordination by distributing the drug in a large volume of air. Alternatively use an inhaler with an automatic release mechanism (e.g. rotahaler). This type of inhaler works by making the release of the drug automatic on reaching sufficient inspiratory pressure.

Joint aspiration

Iatrogenic joint infections are a disaster so an aseptic technique is essential. There are many possible joints that you will be required to aspirate, the commonest being the knee. We have thus concentrated on the knee here but the apparatus and general approach should hold for most joints.

APPARATUS

1 Syringes: 5 ml, 10 ml and 50 ml.

2 Orange (25 G) and green (21 G) needles.

3 Lignocaine 2%.

4 Sterile pack containing drapes, towels, gallipots, cotton wool and gauze.

5 Skin sterilising solution, e.g. Betadine.

6 Specimen containers: sterile for microbiology, fluoride for synovial fluid, glucose and others for biochemistry and protein.

7 Jug for large aspirations.

8 Sterile gloves.

PROCEDURE

1 Explain the procedure to the patient and lie him/her on a bed with leg muscles relaxed.

2 Palpate the borders of the patella and decide, on the basis of anatomy and position of the effusion, whether to approach medially or laterally. Personally we prefer a medial approach in most cases but there are exponents of both. If the effusion is maximal somewhere around the knee, aspirate from this area.

3 Put on gloves and thoroughly clean skin.

4 Infiltrate skin with lignocaine just posterior to the most lateral or most medial border of the patella.

5 Advance the needle posterior to the patella through the synovial membrane, which often presents slight resistance. Anatomically, if the needle is posterior to the patella it must be in the knee joint.

6 Stablilise the needle and syringe and aspirate till almost dry.

7 Send samples to microbiology, biochemistry etc. as required.

You may be required to inject the joint with steroid. The procedure is the same as above except that at the end you need to inject one of the following:

- hydrocortisone 50 mg
- methylprednisolone 40 mg
- triamcinolone 20 mg.

(Doses depend on the joint size — the figures here refer to the knee.)

Liver biopsy

This is a potentially fatal procedure and should not therefore be taken lightly. Watch several being done before attempting one yourself under close supervision. Because of the difficult and dangerous nature of this procedure we have not described how to do it. However you will be responsible for preparing patients and for looking after them post-procedure. We include an apparatus list for use when attempting one yourself.

CONTRA-INDICATIONS
• Prothrombin time more than 3 s longer than control (or INR greater than 1.3).
• Ascites.
• Jaundice.
• Platelet count less than $80\,000 \times 10^9$/litre.
• Uncooperative patients.
• Extrahepatic cholestasis (gallstones, carcinoma of the pancreas).

PREPARATION
1 Consent. Make sure that you explain the risks to the patient and family — see under Consent forms (Chapter 1). Mention the possibility of infection, shoulder pain, bleeding and the need then for a transfusion.
2 Full blood count.
3 Clotting.
4 Give vitamin K injections IV for 3 days if the prothrombin time is abnormal. Check the level again before the test.
5 Group and save.
6 Liver function tests.
7 Ultrasound scan to confirm anatomy.

APPARATUS

1 Biopsy needle (e.g. a Tru-cut or Menghini or Surecut needle (which is a modified Menghini needle).

2 A sterile pack containing gallipots, gauze, cotton wool, sterile towels and drapes.

3 Scalpel blade.

4 Selection of needles: one orange, one blue, one green.

5 Sterile gloves.

6 Cleaning solution — e.g. Betadine.

7 Lignocaine 2% — 5 ml.

8 10 ml syringe.

9 Specimen pots — one containing 20 ml formalin.

10 Indelible ink pen.

AFTER THE PROCEDURE

1 Instruct patient to remain on his or her right side for 4–6 h (most liver biopsies are done as day cases).

2 Perform BP and pulse observations every 30 min for 6 h. Ask staff to alert you if there are any changes in these observations.

3 Ensure the patient has access to analgesia as necessary.

PROBLEMS

• Failure to obtain a specimen: probably the result of incorrect use of the biopsy needle. Never try more than three times.

• Any sign of infection should be treated very aggressively.

• Bleeding.

Lumbar puncture

This is an intricate and delicate procedure which should be learned by watching experienced colleagues: make sure you are closely supervised during your first few. We have listed some basic information to allow you to set yourself up to do lumbar punctures in the future and to allow you to manage the patient before and after the procedure.

CONTRA-INDICATIONS

• Local sepsis.

• Suspicion of intracranial or cord mass.

• Congenital neurological lesions in lumbosacral region.

• Platelet count less than 40×109/litre or other clotting abnormality.

• Unconscious patient with papilloedema.

• Raised intracranial pressure.

• Drowsy patient.

If any of the last three conditions is present, the patient will need an urgent CT scan.

APPARATUS

1 There are normally pre-prepared lumbar puncture packs available which contain lumbar puncture needles, drapes, gallipot, manometer and gauze.

2 Needles: orange (25 G) and green (21 G).

3 10 ml syringe.

4 Lignocaine 2%.

5 Cleaning solution — e.g. Betadine.

6 Up to six sterile specimen pots.

7 Gloves.

After the procedure lie all patients flat for 12 h to reduce the incidence of subsequent headache.

If you suspect meningitis send samples for:

• Microscopy, culture and sensitivity studies

• protein

• glucose

• blood glucose.

For interpretation of results see Chapter 7.

COMPLICATIONS

• Headaches occur in approximately 10% of patients after lumbar puncture. Treat this by lying the patient flat, and giving adequate analgesia, anti-emetics and time. The headache may not begin for 3–4 days.

- Nerve damage.
- Cord damage.
- Infection.
- Coning: if the patient's conscious level deteriorates after a lumbar puncture be alert to the possibility of coning — call help urgently.

Nasogastric intubation

Nursing staff will normally pass wide-bore nasogastric tubes and often fine-bore tubes as well. However if they encounter problems or if they are unable because of hospital nursing regulations to pass fine-bore tubes, the job will be yours. If you are asked to take over the passage of a nasogastric tube that a staff nurse or sister has failed to pass, you're in trouble because they've been doing it for years.

APPARATUS

1 Nasogastric tube. For aspirations use a 16 G tube; and for feeding a fine bore one.
2 Lubricating jelly (some tubes are coated in dried jelly which becomes a lubricant when wet.
3 Gloves — non-sterile.
4 50 ml syringe.
5 Tape.
6 Litmus paper.

PROCEDURE

1 Explain what is required to the patient and sit him/her upright with the neck slightly flexed.
2 Don gloves — the procedure does not need to be sterile but can be messy.
3 Apply jelly to the tube tip (or wet the tube depending on type).

4 Introduce the tube into the patient's nostril and pass backwards along the floor of the nose. Stop as it reaches the nasopharynx.

5 Ask the patient to swallow and simultaneously advance the tube.

6 The stomach should be reached after about 35–40 cm has been passed.

7 Confirm the tube is correctly positioned in the stomach by either: (a) pushing air down the tube with a syringe and listening over the stomach with a stethoscope; (b) aspirating the stomach contents and checking that this fluid is acid with the litmus paper; or (c) obtaining a CXR.

8 If you have any doubts about the position of the tube, perform a CXR (after withdrawing the guide wire if you've inserted a fine-bore tube).

9 Fix the tube securely to the edge of the nose and forehead with tape.

PROBLEMS/PRECAUTIONS

• If the patient begins to choke, withdraw immediately, let the patient recover and try again.

• If the tube is gagged forward into the mouth, withdraw to nasopharynx and re-try. Give the patient a mouthful of water (if not contra-indicated) and time your advance to the swallow. Alternatively, give the patient an anaesthetic lozenge.

• Cooling the tube can make it stiffer and less likely to pass into the mouth.

• An expert may be able to guide the tube down the pharynx with a pair of long forceps.

• If none of the above works, ask for help. If your seniors fail, you may have to resort to passing a fine-bore tube under direct vision using an endoscope.

Fine-bore tubes can be left *in situ* for several weeks. Wide-bore tubes need changing at least weekly.

Paracentesis (ascitic tap)

This may be performed for diagnostic purposes (in which case small volumes are required), or for therapeutic reasons in which case it is usually necessary to withdraw several hundred millilitres of fluid.

APPARATUS

1 Dressing pack.

2 Sterile skin cleaning fluid or alcohol swabs.

3 Various syringes (5 ml for local anaesthesia, 50–100 ml for aspiration).

4 21 G needle for diagnostic taps; for therapeutic taps use an 18 G cannula or a peritoneal dialysis or suprapubic catheter attached to a drainage bag.

5 Lignocaine.

6 Sterile gloves.

7 Specimen containers.

PROCEDURE

Therapeutic taps

1 Ask patient to void bladder.

2 Lie patient supine or slightly over towards side of aspiration.

3 Tap out area of shifting dullness where there are no solid organs. It is usually best to use the iliac fossae away from the inferior epigastric vessels (Fig. 3.4). Avoid previous laparotomy scars.

4 Clean skin.

5 Infiltrate 2–4 ml of lignocaine into the skin and deeper tissues and pause for a minute. Remember to aspirate for blood before each infiltration.

6 Insert the suprapubic catheter or 18 G cannula, withdraw the needle and leave the tubing *in situ* attached to a drainage bag. Do not remove more than 3 litres at any one time as this may cause profound hypotension.

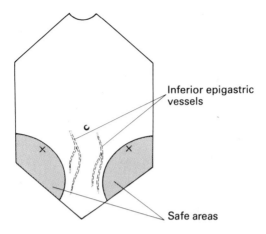

Fig. 3.4 Safe areas to perform paracentesis.

7 You may need to reposition the patient to maintain the flow.

Diagnostic taps
Proceed as above, except that there is often no need for local infiltration of anaesthetic and you should use the 21 G needle. Withdraw about 50 ml and send samples to microbiology (for culture including AAFB), chemical pathology (for glucose and protein), haematology (for WCC) and cytology, as clinical details warrant.

Peripheral cannulae

Setting up a giving set (for IV fluid/drug administration)
The trick is to set up a line without any bubbles:
1 Close the adjustable valve on the giving set (Fig. 3.5).
2 Remove the sterile cover from the bag or bottle outlet.
3 Remove the cover from the giving set connector with a push, twist and a pull. Insert the giving set connector into the bag/bottle with the neck of the bag/bottle upwards and the

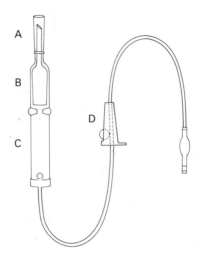

Fig. 3.5 Setting up of a giving set for IV fluid/drug administration. A = plastic cover of connector; B = filter (for blood giving sets); C = drip chamber; D = adjustable valve.

connector downwards. To maintain sterility do not touch the connector with your fingers.

4 Invert the bag to hang on the drip stand and squeeze the drip chamber to obtain a fluid level (Fig. 3.5).

5 Open the adjustable valve partially and allow the fluid to pass down the tubing until it has been filled. If this is done slowly enough you should be able to avoid the formation of bubbles which are annoying and time-consuming to remove.

Removing bubbles

This depends a little on where the bubbles are and whether they are sufficient enough for you to flush the line with more fluid from the bag. If you can't, proceed as follows:

1 *Bubbles near the drip chamber:* Shut the line below the bubbles (e.g. by squeezing the tubing). Hold the line vertically and taut and tap the tubing vigorously (e.g. with the side of a pen) so that the bubbles float up to the chamber.

2 *Bubbles near the distal end:* Disconnect the line from the patient, hold the end upright and tap the bubbles out as described above.

Insertion of a peripheral cannula

A guide to choosing the size of cannula is given in Table 3.2. You will hopefully already be capable of inserting lines into 'good' veins, so we have not detailed the procedure here. However we have listed below a guide to success in difficult situations.

Choosing a vein

The most convenient site is on the left arm 3–5 cm above the wrist (right side for left-handed people). The dorsum of the hand is also useful. Elbow veins should only really be used if there are no veins suitable more distally. Use veins which are palpable, not just visible, and preferably choose a site where two veins join because they are relatively fixed at these points.

If there are no veins visible the following actions may help you make veins more visible or palpable:

1 Sit the patient upright and hang the arm downwards over the edge of the bed to increase the head of pressure.

2 Tap the back of the hand and lower part of the arm or wipe with an alcohol swab.

3 Use a sphygmomanometer. Blow up the cuff to above systolic pressure and leave it inflated for 2 min. This allows a

Table 3.2 Cannula sizes

Size	Colour	Use
22 G	Blue	For small fragile veins
20 G	Pink	For IV drug and fluid administration (if veins are too small for green cannulation)
18 G	Green	Standard size for IV drugs, fluids and blood administration
17 G	Yellow	As for 18 G
16 G	Grey	For any patient requiring rapid IV fluid replacement (e.g. a GI bleed)
14 G	Brown	This is enormous! Rarely used unless dramatic fluid loss needs to be replaced

build-up of lactic acid etc., which causes a reflex vasodilatation. Then partially release the cuff to a pressure just above diastolic which allows blood to flow into the arm but will prevent venous return, thus dilating the veins even further. This method can be very painful so it should only be used when absolutely necessary.

4 If a vein still cannot be found, apply warmth to the back of the hand or wrist (e.g. fill a syringe with warm water or put the patient's hand into a bucket of warm water).

5 As a last resort, apply a GTN patch distally on the arm. There is often a dramatic dilatation of veins further up the arm.

6 Finally, you may be forced to use foot veins. However, it is worth checking with a senior member of your team as many people dislike the use of foot veins especially in patients who are prone to infection or thrombosis (e.g. diabetics).

You may find that the veins are visible but that each time you attempt to insert a line you 'blow' the vein. If this is the case, it is often possible to 'float' the cannula into the vein, as follows:

1 Introduce the tip of the cannula into the vein but advance no further to avoid piercing.

2 Remove the needle, connect a syringe filled with saline or heparinised saline to the cannula and slowly inject fluid into the vein whilst advancing the cannula.

To take blood via a peripheral line
It is often very useful, and more satisfactory from the patient's standpoint, to remove blood at the same time as inserting the cannula. The object is to avoid a mess. Once the cannula has been inserted, block the end under the skin with your thumb as you withdraw the needle. Elevate the arm to a level above the heart to prevent blood flow. Apply a syringe to the cannula outlet, lower the arm and aspirate the amount of blood

required. It may help to withdraw the cannula tubing slightly to facilitate blood flow. Once you have finished, block the vein again, raise the arm and apply a cap. Flush with saline.

Other tips
Shave very hairy arms, since pulling the tape off can be very painful. Tape down all lines well as they are easily and frequently pulled out. Check all of your venflons are working before going to bed!

You may be called to re-site a cannula because it has 'tissued' or the drip has stopped working — always remember that the line can very often be salvaged. If you are called in the middle of the night you will need to decide on the merits of each case whether it is important to re-site the cannula there and then. Circumstances in which it is imperative that the patient has a functional line even at night are:
• IV drug infusions
• inadequate oral fluid intake
• poor urine output
• emergency blood transfusions
• any acutely ill patient.

Pleural aspiration

This may be required for diagnostic or therapeutic purposes.

APPARATUS
There may be pre-packed pleural aspiration sets available containing most of the items on this list:
1 Sterile towels.
2 Skin cleaning fluid (e.g. Betadine).
3 20 ml syringe for diagnostic taps; 50 ml syringe with a Luer-lok for therapeutic taps.
4 Lignocaine 2%.
5 21 G needle for diagnostic taps. A pleural aspiration set

containing needles, trocars and cannulae is preferable for therapeutic taps.

6 Three-way tap.

7 Receiver for fluid (e.g. a jug).

8 Adhesive dressing.

9 Specimen bottles — depending on clinical indications for the procedure.

PROCEDURE

1 Review the CXR and check clinically which side is to be drained.

2 Make sure that the patient is sitting comfortably, preferably leaning slightly forward with arms folded before him or her on a pillow. Leaning the patient over the back of a chair on which s/he is seated the wrong way round, is helpful.

3 Tap out effusion and mark the preferred point of entry with an indelible pen on the posterior chest wall medial to the angle of the scapula, one interspace below the upper limit of dullness to percussion.

4 Clean site thoroughly.

5 Infiltrate a small area of skin with lignocaine.

6 Using a 21 G needle infiltrate chest wall with 2–4 ml of local anaesthetic down to the level of the pleura, running close to the superior border of a rib (so as to avoid the neurovascular bundle which runs along the inferior border of the rib). Always check for blood vessel aspiration.

7 You will know that you have reached the pleural space by aspirating on the syringe before each infiltration to see pleural fluid filling the syringe.

8 To remove large quantities of fluid use a needle with an attached three-way tap; this allows you to empty the syringe without disconnecting it from the needle.

9 Avoid introducing air by ensuring that the three-way tap is shut to the chest wall when emptying the syringe. Check before you start.

10 *Do not* remove more than 1.5 litres of fluid at any one time because of the risk of mediastinal shift with or without pulmonary oedema; 50 ml should suffice for diagnostic purposes.

11 Send samples to microbiology, cytology and chemical pathology.

12 Do a post-procedure CXR.

Measurement of pulsus paradoxus

The term 'pulsus paradoxus' is, strictly speaking, a misnomer because it occurs in normal subjects. Intrathoracic pressure drops during inspiration and this tends to reduce the volume of blood expelled from the heart during systole. Hence the systolic pressure drops. There is thus a phasic difference in systolic pressure between inspiration and expiration which in normal subjects is less than 10 mmHg — referred to as 10 mmHg of paradox. In several cardiorespiratory diseases this paradox may be exaggerated. In severe asthma, for example, the intrathoracic pressure drops excessively because the patient is inspiring against airways resistance. Consequently even less blood is expelled during systole and the paradox is increased.

PROCEDURE

1 Inflate sphygmomanometer cuff above systolic pressure.

2 Slowly deflate the cuff and note the pressure at which the first bruit sounds are heard. As indicated above, these sounds will be heard during expiration (i.e. they are intermittent).

3 Continue to deflate the cuff slowly.

4 Note the pressure at which the sounds become continuous (i.e. are heard during inspiration and expiration).

5 The difference between these two pressures represents the degree of paradox.

Respiratory function tests

There are two forms of respiratory function test that you will have to perform on a regular basis: these are spirometry and peak flow rate.

Spirometry

APPARATUS
1 A vitalograph.
2 Vitalograph paper.
3 Mouthpiece.

PROCEDURE
The success of this procedure is largely dependent on a clear explanation to the patient of what is required.
1 Ensure that the machine is plugged in and set the needle to zero on the graph paper.
2 Demonstrate the sequence of events to the patient.
3 Ask the patient to take a few deep breaths and then, when ready, to breathe in as deeply as possible, to place his or her lips around the mouthpiece, and to breathe out as fast and as hard as possible.
4 As the patient begins to exhale push and hold the record button in.
5 Encourage the patient to keep going until the end of the graph paper is reached and then stop. Release the record button.
6 It is useful to repeat the procedure three times if possible and to take the highest FEV_1 (forced expiratory volume in 1 s) and FVC (forced vital capacity) of the three attempts.
7 Record the expected value in the notes alongside the attained values.

Obstructive picture if:

$$\frac{FEV_1}{FVC} < 75\%$$

Restrictive picture if:

$$\frac{FEV_1}{FVC} > 75\%$$

Peak expiratory flow rate

Measurements are useful for assessing the progress of disease in an individual patient (particularly asthmatics or patients with COAD) and for the pre-operative assessment of patients with respiratory diseases.

Method

1 Ask the patient to take a full inspiration to total lung capacity.

2 Blow out forcefully into the peak flow meter, the lips placed tightly around the mouthpiece.

3 Use the best of three recordings.

4 It is worth recording the expected value in the notes as well as the results achieved.

The PEFR measures the maximum expiratory flow rate in the first 2 ms of expiration.

Expected values for respiratory function tests (Table 3.3–3.5)

Table 3.3 Predicted values for FEV_1 (litres)

(a) Males

Age (years)	Height (m)				
	1.50	1.60	1.70	1.80	1.90
15–20	2.80	3.30	3.55	3.90	4.30
20–25	3.25	3.60	3.95	4.35	4.70
25–35	3.10	3.45	3.80	4.20	4.55
35–45	2.80	3.15	3.50	3.90	4.25
45–55	2.50	2.85	3.20	3.60	3.90
55–65	2.15	2.50	2.90	3.25	3.60
65–75	1.85	2.20	2.60	2.95	3.30
75–80	1.55	1.90	2.25	2.65	3.00
85 +	1.40	1.75	2.10	2.50	2.85

(b) Females

Age	Height (m)				
(years)	1.40	1.50	1.60	1.70	1.80
15–25	2.45	2.80	3.15	3.45	3.75
25–35	2.35	2.65	2.95	3.30	3.65
35–45	2.05	2.35	2.65	3.05	3.35
45–55	1.75	2.05	2.35	2.75	3.05
55–65	1.45	1.75	2.10	2.45	2.75
65–75	1.15	1.45	1.85	2.15	2.45
75–80	0.85	1.20	1.55	1.85	2.15
85 +	0.75	1.05	1.35	1.70	2.05

Table 3.4 Predicted normal values for FVC (litres)

(a) Males

Age	Height (m)				
(years)	1.50	1.60	1.70	1.80	1.90
15–20	3.45	4.00	4.50	5.05	5.55
20–25	3.65	4.15	4.70	5.20	5.75
25–35	3.55	4.05	4.60	5.10	5.60
35–45	3.30	3.85	4.35	4.90	5.40
45–55	3.10	3.60	4.15	4.65	5.20
55–65	2.85	3.40	3.95	4.45	4.95
65–75	2.65	3.15	3.70	4.20	4.75
75–80	2.45	2.95	3.45	4.00	4.50
85 +	2.35	2.85	3.35	3.90	4.40

(b) Females

Age	Height (m)				
(years)	1.50	1.60	1.70	1.80	1.90
15–25	2.90	3.40	3.85	4.35	4.75
25–35	2.75	3.25	3.70	4.15	4.65
35–45	2.45	2.95	3.45	3.90	4.35
45–55	2.20	2.65	3.15	3.60	4.05
55–65	1.90	2.35	2.85	3.30	3.75
65–75	1.60	2.10	2.55	3.00	3.45
75–80	1.30	1.80	2.25	2.70	3.20
85 +	1.20	1.65	2.10	2.60	3.05

Table 3.5 Predicted values for PEFR (litre/min)

(a) Males

Age (years)	Height (m)				
	1.50	1.60	1.70	1.80	1.90
15–20	440	475	510	545	580
20–25	535	570	610	645	680
25–35	525	560	595	630	665
35–45	500	535	570	605	635
45–55	480	510	545	575	610
55–65	455	490	520	550	580
65–75	435	465	495	525	550
75–80	410	440	465	495	525
85 +	410	430	455	480	510

(b) Females

Age (years)	Height (m)				
	1.50	1.60	1.70	1.80	1.90
15–25	360	395	435	470	510
25–35	350	385	420	460	495
35–45	325	365	400	440	475
45–55	305	345	380	420	455
55–65	285	320	360	395	435
65–75	265	300	340	375	415
75–80	245	280	315	355	390
85 +	235	270	305	345	380

Sutures

You will probably only be faced with having to do sutures on skin lesions or when inserting a chest drain or central line etc. If you have never done any stitching get somebody to show you the basics and practise whenever you can. You may be confused about the nomenclature and coding system of the various types of suture available. We have therefore outlined here the basics of suture choice. You will only rarely use many of the types listed below but we have included them to increase your general understanding.

SIZE/GAUGE

The various sizes are ascribed a reference number which indicates the calibre of the suture material. In order of *decreasing* size:

- size 2
- size 1
- size 0
- size 00 referred to as 2/0
- size 000 referred to as 3/0
- size 0000 referred to as 4/0
- size 00000 referred to as 5/0
- size 000000 referred to as 6/0
- size 0000000 referred to as 7/0 etc.

Sizes 2 and 1 are used for coarse tissues where much tensile strength is required — e.g. abdominal or back muscles.

Sizes 0 and 2/0 are suitable for peritoneum, gut and subcutaneous tissues.

Sizes 3/0 and 4/0 are suitable for skin on legs or arms.

Sizes 5/0 and 6/0 should be used for hand and facial stitching.

NB: Metric sizes are also noted on the packaging. Metric size 4 = 0.4 mm width; metric size 3 = 0.3 mm width; etc.

You may hear theatre staff referring to sutures by their re-order numbers. Thus you will hear a request for a size '441'. Ignore this system unless you are likely to be involved in re-ordering.

TYPES OF SUTURE

There are essentially two types of suture: absorbable and non-absorbable.

Absorbable

These materials are broken down by enzymes at varying speeds. Generally used for internal suturing. Examples:

1 Plain catgut

- made from sheep's intestines! Absorbed within 5–10 days
- used for subcutaneous suturing
- very springy, so stretch before using
- keep moist
- colour: light tan.

2 Chromic catgut
- dipped in chromic acid, thus more resistant to digestion
- absorbed in 10–20 days
- handling characteristics similar to plain catgut but less irritant
- colour: brown.

3 Dexon
- A synthetic absorbable suture made of polyglycolic acid
- absorbed in 60–90 days
- easier to handle than catgut
- colour: green or white.

4 Vicryl
- also synthetic — polyglactin 910
- absorbed in 70–80 days
- colour: violet.

Non-absorbable

These may be used internally for tissues that require permanent support or on skin where they will have to be removed after sufficient time for healing. Examples:

1 Ethilon (nylon)
- extra knots are required to prevent slipping
- good tensile strength
- colour: black, green or blue.

2 Prolene
- similar characteristics to Ethilon and similar uses but less irritant
- holds knots better
- colour: blue.

3 Ethibond
  - most commonly used for cardiovascular surgery and for anastomosing blood vessels
  - colour: white or green.

4 Silk
  - easy to handle but not very strong
  - colour: black.

5 Linen
  - limited uses — e.g. in the gut or tying off deep vessels
  - colour: white.

You may hear people referring to monofilament or polyfilament sutures. The main significance of the distinction is that multistranded sutures can allow capillary movement of tissue fluids between the threads, which predisposes to infection. The distinction is unlikely to affect you in the course of day-to-day ward work.

Needles
There are varying shapes of needle; some have sharp points but round smooth bodies whereas others have triangular shaped bodies with cutting edges. For most skin suturing a needle with cutting edges should be used.

Tuberculin testing

These types of test are designed to test an individual's sensitivity to tuberculoprotein, which is a sterile preparation made from heat-treated products of the *Mycobacterium* organism.

The multiple puncture test (Heaf test)

A solution containing 100 000 u/ml is introduced by use of a puncture apparatus.

Apply PPD solution with a sterile rod and spread it over an area of 1 cm^2.

The gun should be sterilised by immersing in methylated spirit
and burning it off if not already autoclaved.

Set it to puncture at a depth of 2 mm for a patient over 2 years
of age (1 mm for patients less than 2 years old).

Apply the head and release the needles. Let the solution dry.
No dressing is needed.

Read the result at 4–7 days.

A positive result should be recorded only when there is
palpable induration around at least four puncture points.
Four grades of response are defined for the Heaf test:

- Grade 1: at least four small indurated papules.
- Grade 2: an indurated ring formed by confluent papules.
- Grade 3: solid induration 5–10 mm wide.
- Grade 4: induration over 10 mm wide.

The Mantoux test

The Mantoux test may be used for routine pre-BCG skin
testing or for diagnostic purposes. During day-to-day ward
work you will be using this test to help diagnose TB in patients
with suspicious symptoms or signs. In these cases, the initial
dose is 1 u of tuberculin PPD in 0.1 ml (dilution 10 u/ml)
injected intradermally with a 25 G needle so that a bleb of
approximately 7 mm is produced. This bleb is usually raised on
the flexor aspect of the forearm after cleaning with spirit. Mark
the patient's arm with an indelible pen to indicate where the
protein was injected. The result should be read after 48–72 h.
A positive result consists of induration of at least 5 mm in
diameter following injection of 0.1 ml of PPD 10 u/ml: redness
without oedema is not positive.

Interpretation of results

According to the Department of Health 1990 guidelines, 'all
those who show a strongly positive reaction to tuberculin
should be referred for further investigation ... A strongly
positive reaction is a Heaf response of Grade 3 or 4 or a

Mantoux response with induration of at least 15 mm diameter following 0.1 ml PPD 100 units/ml.'

Venesection of a unit of blood

APPARATUS
1 Venesection bag with needle and tubing attached — call the haematology department if you can't find one.
2 Orange (25 G) needle.
3 5 ml syringe.
4 2% lignocaine.
5 Tape.
6 Sphygmomanometer.
7 Cotton-wool ball.

PROCEDURE
1 Lie the patient flat.
2 Take a resting BP and pulse.
3 Pump the sphygmomanometer to about 60–80 mmHg.
4 Feel for an antecubital vein.
5 Carefully anaesthetise the area of skin directly over the vein.
6 Once numb, insert the venesection needle and advance fully into the vein. Tape down firmly.
7 Make sure the plastic tubing attached to the needle is unclamped. Blood should begin to drain into the bag quite quickly (15–30 min to fill the bag) — it is often quite difficult to assess whether blood is still flowing.
8 Once the bag is filled to its maximum let the sphygmomanometer down and gently pull the needle out using cotton wool to plug the puncture site.
9 You must hold the plastic tubing and needle upright with the bag on the floor to prevent a blood bath.
10 Cut the needle off and tie the plastic tubing in a knot to prevent haemorrhage.
11 Send the venesected blood to the haematology department.

4: Surgical Considerations

There are widely differing views on which antibiotics to use prophylactically, when to give them and how long to use them for post-operatively. Similarly the correct prophylactic use of heparin is also disputed. You may conclude that whatever decision you make, it turns out to be the wrong one. To save much irritation and frustration it is advisable to sit down and chat with your registrar or senior registrar on your first day as a surgical house officer to establish their preferences for 'working up' a patient for each particular operation.

Pre-operative checklist

Your role in preparing a patient for the operating theatre is administrative. You have to ensure that all the necessary blood tests and X-rays have been done; that the patient has consented suitably to the operation; that they have had their pre-operative antibiotics; that the 'pre-med' has been prescribed etc. If you are busy it is easy to forget something essential and then comes one of those terrifying calls from theatre asking why something hasn't been done. The only way around this is to have an extensive checklist to run through. We have outlined such a list (Table 4.1) which we hope covers most of what is necessary. We suggest you photocopy it and attach it to the front of all your patients' notes.

Most patients going to theatre for routine operations are medically well and it is easy to become blasé about your history-taking and examination — *Don't*! You have an important role in deciding whether or not your patient is fit for an operation. An anaesthetist will check the patient pre-operatively but this may only happen very shortly before they

Table 4.1 Pre-operative checklist

	Job done	Results in notes?		Job done?
			3 Procedures completed (as necessary)	....
1 General				
FBC	....	....	Patient catheterised?	....
U & Es	....	....	ITU/HDU bed booked?	....
G & S/CM	....	....	Operation site marked?	....
CXR	....	....	Anaesthetic sheets completed?	....
ECG	....	....	Special arrangements?	....
Consent	....	....	Frozen section arranged?	....
Anaesthetist informed?	....		LFTs?	....
Operation list complete?	....			
2 Specifics			**4 Prescriptions written-up** (as necessary)	
Sickle screen	....	....	Antibiotics	....
Clotting screen	....	....	SC heparin	....
Arterial blood gas	....	....	Pre-op. overnight fluids	....
Other details	....	....	Pre-med	....
			Bowel preparation given	....
			Steroids	....
			Insulin infusion	....

are due to go to theatre. If there is an obvious problem you will look foolish if you have missed it. Until you become familiar with the preferences of different anaesthetists contact them if there is *anything* you are worried or unsure about.

The condition of postoperative patients can change incredibly quickly — involve your seniors sooner rather than later even if there has only been a small change.

Group and Save or Cross Match?

In Table 4.2 we have listed guidelines for G & S or CM requirements for reference, bearing in mind that each firm has its own ideas about what is needed.

Table 4.2 Group and Save or Cross Match?

	G & S or CM?	
Operation	**Advised**	**Your team's preferences**
Hepatobiliary		
PTC/liver biopsy	G & S	....
ERCP	G & S	....
Liver/pancreas	6	....
GIT/abdomen		
Pyloric stenosis	G & S	....
Oesophagectomy	4	....
Gastrectomy	2	....
Cholecystectomy	G & S	....
Splenectomy	2	....
Ileal reservoir	2	....
Appendicectomy	G & S	....
Colectomy	2	....
Abdominoperineal	4	....
Hernia	Nil	....
Prostatectomy	2	....
Vascular		
Aneurysm (elective)	6	....
Aneurysm (emergency)	10	.... *NB*: may need platelets
Aortobifemoral	6	....
Femoropopliteal	2	....
Carotid endarterectomy	2	....

Table 4.2 *(continued)*

Operation	G & S or CM? Advised	Your team's preferences
Amputation	G & S	....
Varicose veins	G & S	....
Orthopaedic Total hip replacement	4	....
Hemi-arthroplasty	2	....
Dynamic hip screw	2	....
Arthroscopy	Nil	....

Others (fill in as they arise)

....

....

....

....

....

Figures refer to the required number of units of whole blood for cross matching.

5: Cardiac Arrests

Cardiopulmonary resuscitation — policy guidelines

Is this patient for 'crash', Doctor?

Unless previously decided, all patients on the ward are for active resuscitation should the need arise. To decide whether or not a patient is for active resuscitation, may at first seem rather god-like. It is a decision which should never be taken lightly and preferably not by a newly qualified house officer. In some hospitals there is a policy that on admission all patients should be categorised ('resus.' or 'not for resus.') by a senior member of staff.

Usually, if a patient is sick the team will decide, after discussion with nursing staff, relatives and possibly the patient him/herself, whether or not they feel that active resuscitation is appropriate. It is the nursing staff who are usually present when a patient arrests and for their own professional safety the decision should be clearly written in the notes.

If the decision *is not* clearly documented, patients with end-stage terminal diseases will be 'crashed'. This is a disaster for all concerned — a peaceful death can be turned into a melodramatic death and the arrest team will be somewhat annoyed to be called out unnecessarily — so make this a priority of yours. Note, however, that there are consultants who are reluctant for various reasons to have these decisions documented in the notes — so check the policy of your firm.

There is an important distinction to be made between 'not for cardiopulmonary resuscitation' and 'not for active management'. If the decision has been taken *not* to resuscitate a patient in the event of a cardiac or respiratory arrest this does *not* mean that nothing should be done for the patient in the event of their becoming acutely ill. Many patients only benefit from

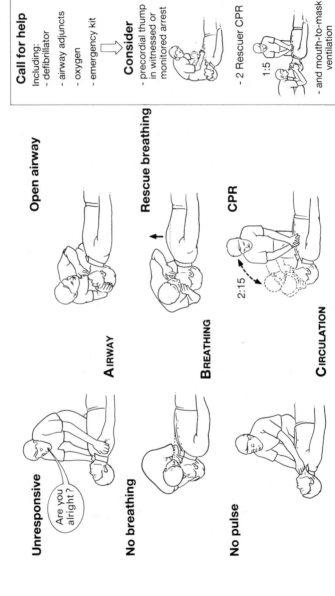

Unresponsive

Are you alright?

No breathing

No pulse

AIRWAY

Open airway

BREATHING

Rescue breathing

CIRCULATION

CPR

2:15

Call for help

Including:
- defibrillator
- airway adjuncts
- oxygen
- emergency kit

Consider
- precordial thump in witnessed or monitored arrest

- 2 Rescuer CPR

1:5

- and mouth-to-mask ventilation

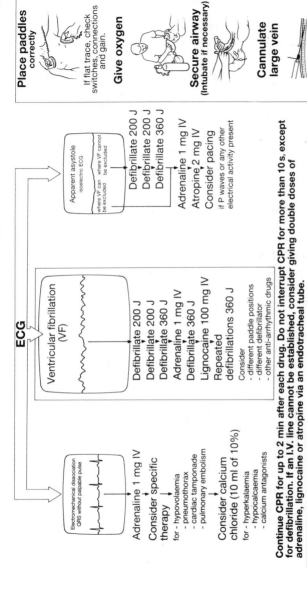

Fig. 5.1 Protocol for the treatment of cardiac arrest cases in hospital. From leaflet produced by Leardal Medical Ltd and The Resuscitation Council (UK).

aggressive active management. Often a house officer is called to see a patient s/he doesn't know, notices that a decision has been made not to crash the patient has been taken and avoids all treatment. This is wrong and the distinction here must be appreciated.

If you are in a crisis situation and there is any doubt in your mind then you should always crash the patient. You may find yourself pressurised by ward staff to make a decision. If there is time, contact the on-call medical registrar and ask for advice, and if you're not happy, *crash the patient.*

What to do at a cardiac arrest (Fig. 5.1)

Your job at arrests is to:

1 Ensure that an airway has been secured and oxygen is being correctly administered: leave 'the head end' to the anaesthetist once s/he arrives.

2 Ensure that the basics of effective massage are under way.

3 Secure IV access.

There is no point in worrying about drug administration to revive the heart if the basics are not being done because cerebral anoxia will make your efforts futile.

NOTES

1 Put on a pair of gloves.

2 Before you have obtained a monitor reading through the applied chest leads you can obtain a readout by placing the defibrillator paddles on the chest.

3 Treat 'sharps' with the same degree of respect during an arrest as at any other time.

4 If you are dealing with an arrest brought in from the community by emergency ambulance, there may be surplus staff around. If so, it is often very useful for somebody to be gathering as much information as possible from any witnesses or relatives, such as the patient's general health, the drugs they take and events leading up to the collapse.

5 Find out on day 1 of your job how the defibrillator works and get to know your hospital's arrest trolley.

6 An air of quiet, calm efficiency should prevail and you will have an important role in ensuring that this is the case.

7 There should be only one chief and lots of indians — it is important to establish exactly who is in charge.

8 Other patients on the ward can hear through the curtains so take care to communicate in a professional manner at all times — it is easy for the whole situation to develop into a circus and to forget those around you.

9 If you run to an arrest, but despite great effort the patient dies, never be flippant as you sit and discuss what has gone on — the nursing staff may be much closer emotionally to the patient than yourself and will be offended by your attitude.

10 Get into the habit of noting the time as soon as the 'arrest bleep' goes off so that you can keep track of how long CPR has continued.

11 Go to bed with the ability to react quickly in the event of your bleep going off — time really does matter.

6: Common Calls

This section is not intended to be a text on the precise, specific management of particular conditions. However it *is* here to help you deal calmly with the more common clinical problems that the ward staff will call you to deal with. We have tried to encourage a systematic approach to the patient to help you make a diagnosis and initiate special investigations and basic management, so that when you do call your registrar or senior house officer, you will have at least done something useful.

When called from your bed at night to deal with a problem, obtain as much information as you can over the phone if time permits. Whilst getting up and walking over to the ward you can thus ponder over the causes of the problem on the basis of the facts you have been presented with. As a general rule, don't decide on management on the basis of single readings.

No matter how tired you are, there is no point getting annoyed with whoever rings you — if you alienate them they will ring you *more* often. If you get on with them they have probably already considered whether or not they could safely leave you in bed. If you feel that the call is pointless, check that the night sister is aware of the problem and see if she feels it is necessary for you to go to the ward. Remember that when a nurse calls you, the call is documented in the nursing records as 'doctor informed' — the responsibility for not going to the ward is then yours.

Poor urine output

'This patient has only passed 50 ml of urine in the past 6 hours.'

You will receive calls such as this on many occasions, especially from surgical wards. Remember that a patient should pass on average not less than 0.5 ml of urine/kg/h. Thus for a 70 kg patient 35 ml/h is the minimum output. Any less than 20 ml/h requires urgent assessment (i.e. getting out of bed) since renal failure may be impending. Consider catheterising all patients passing less than 400 ml of urine in 24 h: (a) to allow accurate assessment of output; and (b) to exclude certain postrenal causes.

SYSTEMATIC PROBLEM APPROACH
Causes of poor urine output may be: postrenal; prerenal; or renal.

Postrenal causes
These must be excluded first in all patients with unexplained poor urine output. The common causes whilst a patient is in hospital are:
1 Blocked urinary catheter.
2 Postoperative urinary retention — exacerbated by benign prostatic hypertrophy.

Prerenal causes
Under this heading comes any condition which causes a reduction in renal blood flow, e.g.:
1 Volume depletion: diarrhoea and vomiting, previously poly-uric, inadequate fluid replacement in postoperative patients.
2 Shock: Haemorrhage, septicaemia.
3 Cardiac failure.
4 Severe hepatic failure.

Renal causes
Renal problems are the least likely cause of poor urine output. Of those causes due to an intrinsic renal problem, 75% are due to ATN, which is reversible.

PATIENT ASSESSMENT

The initial information you will need is as follows:

1 How many millilitres of urine have been passed in the last 24 h?

2 Is the bladder palpable or not (i.e. is the patient in acute urinary retention)?

3 If a catheter is *in situ* and the bladder is thought to be palpable, has a bladder washout been done? If not then ask the nursing staff to do one and to phone you back if no urine is produced.

4 Has the patient failed to urinate despite standing up and listening to a running tap *and* are they in discomfort? If so they should be catheterised.

ON ARRIVAL

1 Is the patient volume depleted or not:

  (a) fluid losses greater than input. Beware of hidden losses such as unmeasured diarrhoea, insensible losses from a pyrexia;

  (b) very concentrated urine. Check specific gravity by use of Dip-stix;

  (c) postural hypotension—a drop in BP of more than 20 mmHg or a systolic drop to less than 100 mmHg on standing;

  (d) low or negative CVP;

  (e) looks dry (check skin turgor and moistness of tongue).

2 If you have excluded a postrenal cause for the problem, you feel certain that the patient is volume depleted and they are *not* in heart failure then you should try a fluid challenge: Give 1 u of colloid (e.g. Haemaccel) over 30 min. If this fails to improve the urine output and cardiac reserve will allow, repeat the challenge.

3 If there is good evidence that the problems are due to LVF or RVF then diuretics can be used (e.g. 40 mg frusemide IV). If you have misinterpreted the situation this action will of course make things worse.

4 If either of these two simple measures fails to work or you are uncertain as to the cause of the poor urine output you should call for help.

5 Meanwhile you should carry out the following:

  (a) urgent microscopy of the urine;

  (b) urgent U & E and creatinine assessment;

  (c) measure the urinary sodium concentration and/or osmolality;

  (d) Dip-stix urine for specific gravity, protein etc.

Remember that in prerenal renal failure the healthy kidney retains salt and water so that:

1 The urine will be concentrated.

2 Urine is of high osmolality and sodium concentration is less than 20 mmol/l.

3 The urine : plasma concentration ratio is more than 8 : 1 for urea and more than 40 : 1 for creatinine.

In ATN there is:

1 Severe oliguria.

2 Mild proteinuria.

3 Urinary sodium concentration greater than 50 mmol/l.

Gastrointestinal bleeding

Any call to say that a patient has vomited fresh or altered blood or passed malaena or fresh blood per rectum should be taken seriously because there is a very real potential for rapid deterioration.

There are a few pertinent questions you could ask when phoned about a patient with GI bleeding, the answers to which you can be pondering over whilst walking to the ward.

PATIENT ASSESSMENT

The initial information you need is:

1 The degree of hypotension and tachycardia — since this reflects on how quickly you should be stepping out of bed.

2 Is there haematemesis and malaena? Does the haematemesis resemble coffee-grounds or is it fresh blood?

3 Is this a new problem?

4 Does the patient have IV access? If so ask the nurses to commence an IV infusion of colloid (e.g. Haemaccel) if the bleed is significant.

The initial management of all patients with GI bleeding should be the same; the degree of urgency is dependent on the severity of the clinical picture.

ON ARRIVAL

Decide on the degree of severity. It is severe if:

1 features of shock are present — pallor, sweating, peripherally shut down;

2 systolic blood pressure is less than 100 mmHg;

3 Pulse rate is over 100/min (may not happen in patients on beta-blockers).

If the patient is not shocked then you probably have more time to play with to make a definitive diagnosis with a thorough history and examination (including a pr examination).

INITIAL MANAGEMENT

1 Assess the actual blood loss (often very difficult).

2 Reassure the patient and staff.

3 Tilt the head of the bed down. Ensure a sucker is available to prevent the patient aspirating blood.

4 Instigate quarter-hourly observations.

5 Gain IV access — a peripheral grey or brown venflon if possible. Central line insertion is indicated if:

   (a) there have been repeated episodes of bleeding;

   (b) the patient is elderly;

   (c) there is a history of cardiac disease.

6 Restore the circulating blood volume — see below.

7 Consider transfer to ITU/HDU or a comparably equipped ward.

8 Perform the following tests:

(a) FBC. The haemoglobin is of only limited value in assessing the degree of current bleeding, before haemodilution has occurred. However, if the haemoglobin at this stage is already low, having been previously normal, this is obviously very significant;

(b) U & E and creatinine. Remember that the urea may be raised as a result of the absorption of blood from the GI tract as well as meaning volume depletion;

(c) cross-match 4 units — 6 units if dealing with bleeding varices;

(d) ECG;
(e) CXR; } non-urgently

(f) clotting studies;

(g) LFTs non-urgently.

9 Ask for an accurate fluid balance chart to be kept, and ask the nurses to contact you if:

(a) there is further siginificant haemorrhage (more than 200 ml);

(b) pulse rate is greater than 100/min;

(c) encephalopathy;

(d) systolic BP is less than 100 mmHg;

(e) oliguria.

10 Keep the patient NBM for 12 h initially; if however s/he continues to bleed or there is a high likelihood that s/he will proceed to surgery then keep the patient NBM. Remember also that any patient proceeding to endoscopy should be NBM for the previous 8 h.

11 *Always* contact your registrar.

12 *Always* contact the on-call endoscopist to make him or her aware of the situation, since all patients with GI bleeding should be scoped within 24 h of the first bleed, and earlier endoscopy is often appropriate.

13 If there is evidence of continued bleeding or recurrent bleeding — *always* contact the duty surgical team.

RESTORATION OF CIRCULATING VOLUME

The aim is to restore the arterial pressure and pulse to normal by replacing the volume of blood that has been lost. However it is often difficult to assess the loss accurately and you will often have to depend on regular reassessment to ensure that the patient is clinically improving. If you have a central line *in situ* then aim to keep the CVP readings in the mid to low normal range (there is a certain risk of promoting a re-bleed if the CVP is too high).

Always get blood as soon as possible but in the meantime use colloid.

SUGGESTED PROTOCOL

Run in 500 ml Haemaccel (or equivalent) over the first half-hour — or faster if failing to maintain the BP. If this brings the BP up, then continue with 0.9% sodium chloride running at a rate that is titrated against the BP. Slow down the infusion as soon as the patient is stable.

If the BP is, however, continuing to fall use Haemaccel until the blood arrives. In desperate circumstances use 'O' negative blood or uncross-matched blood of the patient's group.

Notes

1 Volumes of more than 1000 ml colloid may theoretically cause DIC. Therefore get blood as soon as possible.
2 Patients with poor liver function and oesophageal varices may have ascites which can be worsened by the concurrent administration of sodium chloride (a major component of Haemaccel); thus stick to 5% dextrose in these patients if at all possible.
3 Watch out for signs of heart failure.

Hypertension

1 There is no normal BP except in the statistical sense.

2 Always compare the current reading with the patient's usual BP.

3 This is usually a chronic condition but *must* be considered to be an emergency in the following situations:

(a) when it is causing LVF;

(b) in hypertensive encephalopathy: headache, deterioration in vision, proteinuria and retinal haemorrhage;

(c) in association with a dissecting aortic aneurysm;

(d) in association with an acute or chronic renal failure.

In these circumstances a medical registrar should be involved to oversee the safe administration of antihypertensives.

4 In uncomplicated hypertension, discuss management with colleagues if possible. If it is the middle of the night give a stat dose of 10–20 mg of nifedipine and review the situation in the morning.

NB: Avoid treating patients with hypertension for at least 24–48 h after a cerebrovascular accident.

Pre-operative hypertension

Many anaesthetists would be unhappy about anaesthetising patients with diastolic pressures above 100 mmHg. With stunning regularity this comes to light an hour before the patient is due to go to theatre, and whilst it is best to control the BP for 48 h before the operation, it is often useful to prescribe 10 mg of nifedipine SL. This drug begins to lower the BP within 2 min and has maximal effect within 30–40 min. The dose can be repeated to keep the BP down.

Postoperatively a decision should be made as to the patient's need for long-term antihypertensive treatment.

Postoperative hypertension

Inadequate control of pain postoperatively may well induce a tachycardia and hence a degree of hypertension. Opioid analgesics will reduce pain and also have the advantage, in these circumstances, of reducing BP.

Hypotension (Table 6.1)

This is only clinically significant if the arterial pressure fails to maintain adequate perfusion of vital organs (especially the kidneys and the brain). Hence a systolic pressure of more than 80 mmHg (but higher if the patient was previously hypertensive) is essential. Go and assess all patients with reported hypotension urgently. Whilst walking over to the ward, ask the nursing staff to repeat the vital observations and to do a ward glucose assay.

ON ARRIVAL

1 Always, always recheck the BP yourself. Note the previous readings and assess the degree of fall in BP. Check whether the patient has recently had any sort of procedure leading to a vasovagal attack. In these circumstances the pulse falls instead of rising. Also note if the patient has recently received any anti-hypertensive drugs (e.g. ACE-inhibitors) or analgesia.

2 If there is a tachycardia and significant hypotension then the patient is usually unwell and requires urgent investigation and treatment.

3 The next move really does depend on whether you feel confident with this potentially fatal situation. You must be able to act quickly and intelligently in making a diagnosis and instigating initial management. Tachycardia may not be present in those patients who are on beta-blockers.

4 If you do not feel confident then you *must* call your registrar and start gathering various pieces of information:

   (a) start quarter-hourly observations;

   (b) tilt head end of bed down;

(c) establish venous access;

(d) apply 40% oxygen mask if there are no contra-indications to this.

(e) Take blood for:
- FBC
- clotting screen
- U & E, creatinine and blood glucose
- G & S (if bleeding, cross-match 4 u of packed cells initially; 6 u if dealing with bleeding varices)
- blood cultures;

(f) perform an ECG;

(g) arrange a portable CXR;

(h) if time permits, insert a bladder catheter;

(i) if the problem is blood loss commence colloid replacement — see above under Gastrointestinal bleeding.

Table 6.1 Treatment groups for patients with hypotension

Blood replacement	Peptic ulceration, recent operation, leaking aortic aneurysm
Colloid	Septic shock, dehydration
Steroids	Adrenocortical insufficiency, anaphylactic shock
Inotropes	Cardiogenic shock

Shortness of breath

'Mrs Y is becoming increasingly short of breath.'

The major things to decide over the phone are:

1 Is the patient ill?

2 The severity of the tachypnoea (more than 30 respirations per minute is very significant).

3 Has this been gradual or sudden in onset?

4 Is there any associated chest pain, pyrexia, wheezing?

Five major causes which must be considered:

1 Acute LVF.

2 Acute asthma.

3 Pneumothorax.

4 Pulmonary embolus.
5 Pneumonia.

Whilst walking to the ward ask the nurses to repeat pulse, BP, respiratory rate and a peak flow reading. They will usually have already sat the patient up and applied a 24% oxygen mask.

ON ARRIVAL

You should perform as thorough a history and examination as the clinical situation will allow. Once the patient has been examined, it is pertinent to:

- achieve venous access
- perform arterial blood gas sampling
- arrange a CXR
- carry out an ECG.

CARDINAL SIGNS OF THE FIVE MAJOR CAUSES OF SHORTNESS OF BREATH

LVF

Tachypnoea, tachycardia, gallop rhythm, third heart sound, sweaty, cold, peripherally shut down, pink frothy sputum, fine inspiratory crackles throughout lung fields.

Severe acute asthma

- Pulse more than 120/min.
- PEFR less than 100/min.
- P_{CO_2} more than 6.7 kPa. (More than 5.0 kPA is worrying.)
- Significant degree of pulsus paradox (>10 mmHg).
- Respiratory rate — more than 30/min.
- Patient unable to speak in sentences.

Pneumothorax

This is particularly likely if the patient has recently had a central line inserted. Small ones may be difficult to pick up clinically. Look for absence of lung shadows on an expiratory CXR.

Pulmonary embolus

This is likely if the patient is postoperative and has recently started mobilising. Signs are dependent on the size of the PE:

1 Pleuritic chest pain indicating pulmonary infarction.

2 Cyanosis.

3 Tachypnoea.

4 Tachycardia.

5 Hypotension.

6 Signs of acute right heart strain such as raised JVP, sudden rise in CVP.

7 ECG changes: deep S wave in lead I; Q wave in lead III; inverted T wave in lead III; and V 1–4 or prominent R wave in V1–2. Compare with previous ECGs.

8 ABG showing a hypoxic respiratory alkalosis (i.e. low P_{O_2}, low P_{CO_2} associated with a raised blood pH).

Pneumonia

Tachypnoea, tachycardia, pyrexia, cyanosis, respiratory crackles, bronchial breathing etc.

Chest pain

All chest pain should be taken seriously since it is a symptom in a number of potentially fatal illnesses. Simple angina responds rapidly to SL GTN but other pains may be difficult to sort out. If you are contacted about a patient who has chest pain, try to establish the following points whilst you are on the phone:

1 How ill is the patient? Ascertain the temperature, BP and pulse.

2 Has the patient had this sort of pain before and has this pain responded to GTN previously?

3 Is the pain associated with a tachypnoea?

Whilst walking over to the ward run through a list of the major causes of chest pain (Table 6.2) which are differentiated

Table 6.2 Causes of chest pain

MI
Angina
PE
Aortic aneurysm
Aortic dissection
Gastritis/oesophagitis
Costochondritis
Pericarditis
Pleurisy
Herpes zoster
Abdominal conditions: cholecystitis, pancreatitis, perforated duodenal ulcer/gastric ulcer
Vertebral collapse

on the basis of a history, examination and special investigations. If the patient is also short of breath, cross-refer to the preceding section.

ON ARRIVAL

1 Decide whether the patient is shocked or not — pale, sweaty, peripherally cyanosed with a rapid pulse and low BP.

2 If shocked they are near death and so it is important to call the medical registrar. Whilst s/he is on the way, carry out the following:

   (a) obtain venous access;

   (b) take basic bloods including ABG.

   (c) Perform an ECG. This is vitally important; never miss it out.

   (d) Arrange a portable CXR.

   (e) Set up an ECG monitor if necessary.

If the patient is not shocked a careful history and examination with an accompanying ECG and CXR can usually limit the diagnosis to two or three possibilities: call for help if this is not the case.

Diarrhoea (Table 6.3)

It is all too easy to reach for your pen and write the patient up for an antidiarrhoeal medication just for peace and quiet. In theory, at least, you should establish what is meant by diarrhoea, whether there are any associated symptoms and the duration of the condition.

If the diagnosis is unclear and the diarrhoea has lasted more than a week (which shouldn't be the case for an inpatient), then thorough examination is required — including a rectal examination to rule out faecal impaction. You should then investigate the causes as follows:

1 Send stool samples (× 3) to the laboratory for microscopy to detect ova, cysts and parasites, for culture, and for *Clostridium difficile* toxin.

2 If cultures are negative then consider sigmoidoscopy with rectal biopsy, with or without radiological studies (in that order).

Table 6.3 Major causes of diarrhoea to consider

Acute
Infective:
  Food poisoning
  Viral
Pseudomembranous colitis — particularly in patients on antibiotics
Drugs
Inflammatory bowel disease

Chronic
Inflammatory bowel disease
Parasitic/fungal infections
Malabsorption
Drugs
Diverticular disease
Colonic neoplasia
Endocrine:
  Diabetic neuropathy
  Thyrotoxicosis
  Pancreatic tumours
Faecal impaction
Irritable bowel disease

You should ensure that the patient does not become dehydrated. You can always place him or her on an oral rehydration regimen — see under Oral drugs (Chapter 2) — if oral fluids will suffice. If not, you should commence an IV drip. Also consider employing symptomatic relief with the use of antidiarrhoeals:

1 Loperamide 4 mg initially then 2 mg with each loose stool to a maximum of 16 mg in 24 h. This drug has the advantage of leading to fewer CNS side-effects, *or*

2 Codeine phosphate 30 mg 6 hourly.

Care must be taken in prescribing antidiarrhoeals since they are potentially dangerous in:

1 Colitic attacks because of the risk of perforation and/or toxic megacolon.

2 Infective diarrhoea because they may impair the clearance of the pathogen from the bowel and delay resolution.

NOTES
1 Involve the infection control team.
2 Consider barrier nursing.
3 Make sure you wash your hands between patients!

Persistent nausea and vomiting

You can probably accept one episode of vomiting but should the vomiting persist and be associated with other symptoms you should assess the patient. By knowing the major causes of vomiting, you can narrow the diagnosis by a thorough history and examination. Management will depend on the diagnosis made but in most cases there is a place for symptomatic treatment with an IM or IV anti-emetic.

Don't forget to examine the hernial orifices carefully and record the examination of bowel sounds and pr examination in the notes. Always exclude intestinal obstruction or paralytic ileus. Investigations should be guided by the most likely diagnosis (Table 6.4).

Table 6.4 Major causes of nausea and vomiting

Any GI disease
Acute infections
CNS diseases:
   Raised intracranial pressure
   Meningitis
   Vestibular disturbances
   Pertussis
Metabolic causes
Drugs
Reflex — severe pain such as an MI
Psychogenic
Pregnancy

If a surgical cause is found (e.g. intestinal obstruction), inform the surgeons and then:

1 Keep the patient NBM.

2 Obtain venous access.

3 Perform basic investigations — U & E is important to assess the effect of the vomiting on sodium and potassium levels.

4 Insert a nasogastric tube.

Acute abdominal pain (Table 6.5)

There are a few diagnoses which must be quickly excluded by you — the remaining causes, although potentially serious, do not warrant immediate intervention. It is wise to go and see any patient with severe abdominal pain urgently.

Whilst walking over to the ward you should ask the nursing staff to:

1 Refrain from giving analgesia.

2 Initiate half-hourly observations.

3 Do a ward glucose assay.

4 Keep the patient NBM.

ON ARRIVAL

1 Establish that the patient is not shocked (pale, sweaty,

hypotensive, tachycardic) and that s/he does require immediate resuscitation.

2 If the patient is not shocked your first aim is to exclude:

(a) Peritonism — characterised by fever, guarding, rebound tenderness, and absence of bowel sounds. If generalised, the abdomen will be board-like.

(b) Obstruction — characterised by absolute constipation (no flatus, no bowel motion), colicky abdominal pain, vomiting and abdominal distension.

This can be done by a thorough history and examination and some basic investigations:

1 FBC, to measure the degree of white-cell response and as a preoperative assessment.

2 G & S (cross-match as appropriate).

3 U & E, calcium, glucose and amylase.

4 MSU for the presence of blood or protein and for microscopy and culture — Dip-stix prior to being sent to the laboratory.

5 Plain abdominal supine film and erect CXR.

6 ABG if pancreatitis is suspected.

Always remember that there are extra-abdominal causes of acute abdominal pain including uncontrolled diabetes, basal pneumonia, shingles and MI.

Table 6.5 Major causes of acute abdominal pain

Peritonism
Perforated viscus
Acute cholecystitis
Acute diverticulitis
Acute pancreatitis
Leaking abdominal aortic aneurysm

Obstruction
Adhesions
Herniae
Tumour

NB: Those patients admitted for exacerbation of ulcerative colitis who continue to have abdominal pain should always be investigated for the possibility that they are developing a *toxic megacolon*. This is particularly likely if they have:

1 Fever.
2 Tachycardia greater than 90/min.
3 Abdominal pain.
4 AXR showing dilated colon (more than 10 cm).
5 Rising white cell count.
6 ESR greater than 30 mm/h.

If you feel that this is the case, contact your registrar, who may well speak to the surgeons.

Pyrexia

'This patient is pyrexial.'

This is a problem that you will constantly be faced with. If the patient is not immunocompromised and is systemically well (i.e. normotensive, not sweaty or delirious) then this probably does not require a priority visit to the ward. If the patient is *otherwise well*, you can often allow for a pyrexia of up to 38°C in the following circumstances:

1 Up to 24 h postoperatively.
2 Concurrently receiving a blood transfusion.
3 Recent start (up to 24 h) of a course of antibiotics for a known infection.

If any of the above apply, treat the pyrexia symptomatically with 1 g of paracetamol po/pr and fan the patient.

When you go to assess the patient, your aim will be to find a cause for the pyrexia and initiate treatment if the above circumstances do not account for the problem. The main causes to consider are dependent on the circumstances:

1 Early postoperative period: pulmonary collapse with secondary chest infection or UTI.
2 Late postoperative period: DVT, PE, wound infections.

3 Non-postoperative patients: UTI and chest infections, alcohol withdrawal.

HISTORY
Particularly ask about: diarrhoea with or without blood; cough; dysuria; haematuria; loin pain. It is often useful to ask quickly about sore throat, headache, abdominal pain, painful joints and travel abroad.

EXAMINATION
1 Re-check the oral temperature.
2 Look at the temperature chart to see the pyrexia pattern; e.g. swinging pyrexia suggests a collection of pus.
3 Particularly look for signs of an ENT, respiratory, urinary or wound infection.

SPECIAL INVESTIGATIONS
1 Samples to microbiology:
  • MSU — Dip-stix before sending for MC & S because the presence of blood and protein suggests infection
  • sputum sample
  • stool sample
  • blood cultures
  • swab from any wound
  • also, if indicated, send samples of ascitic fluid, pleural fluid, effusions from joints and CSF.
2 Samples to haematology: FBC — see whether there has been a white cell response. Ask for a white cell differential count: neutrophilia suggests a bacterial infection and lymphocytosis suggests a viral infection. Ask for a 'thick film' to examine for malarial parasites if the patient has been abroad to a high-risk area.
3 Arrange a CXR particularly if there are any localising chest symptoms or signs.

Clinical examination and preliminary investigation will nearly always suggest the most likely diagnosis, which can be treated appropriately. If the likely diagnosis is unclear and the patient is well, you should contact your senior house officer or registrar, who will probably adopt a 'wait and see' policy, being guided by subsequent clinical developments and results from microbiology.

Notes

1 Don't forget non-infectious causes of pyrexia, e.g. MI, DVT, lymphoma and other malignancies, alcoholic hepatitis and toxic megacolon in ulcerative colitis. However, in *all* cases infection should be excluded.

2 A fever of more than 40°C must be taken very seriously because it may cause an encephalopathy and is therefore potentially fatal. Re-check the temperature yourself and, if still high, initiate paracetamol and fanning treatments and ask the on-call medical registrar for instructions on a safe cooling method.

Immunocompromised patients

Any patient with a neutrophil count of less than $1 \times 10^9/l$ or a total WCC of less than $2 \times 10^9/l$ or who has AIDS and develops a pyrexia should be assessed urgently because septic shock and death may ensue rapidly.

1 After quickly completing a full history and examination you should take the following specimens for culture: blood from peripheral veins (and a central line if one is present); stool; sputum (including culture for acid-fast bacilli); nasal swab; throat swab; MSU; and wound swabs (including the site around a Hickman line).

2 Blood tests to be done:
- FBC to confirm the degree of neutropenia and to assess the degree of anaemia and platelet count
- U & E to define the state of renal function should you want to initiate nephrotoxic antibiotics.

3 Always arrange a portable CXR.

4 Consider reverse-barrier nursing if not already in place.

If the patient is unwell then broad-spectrum antibiotics should be initiated *after* all the cultures listed above have been taken. It is likely that your unit will have a preferred broad-spectrum regimen. This is an example:

• Piperacillin and gentamicin plus or minus metronidazole. Flucloxacillin should be incorporated if staphylococcal infection is likely.

• High-dose cephalosporins may be used if the patient is allergic to penicillin.

If these antibiotics fail to settle the pyrexia or improve the patient's condition then you should consider infections other than bacterial ones — e.g. viral, fungal, or parasitic. Always involve senior members of your firm in the management of immunocompromised patients.

If you have managed to isolate a causative organism change your antibiotic as sensitivity studies indicate.

Blood transfusions and reactions to blood transfusions

Remember to take a sample for ferritin, B_{12} and folate assay before starting a transfusion — if time permits.

Top-up transfusions

These are non-urgent transfusions for patients who are chronically anaemic but now symptomatic. They shouldn't be cross-matched during 'on call' hours or weekends.

As a rough guide, each unit of packed cells will raise the haemoglobin by about 1 g/dl. These transfusions should be given over about 3–4 h per unit. In the elderly, or those with poor cardiac reserve, it is wise to administer 20 mg of frusemide po before the first unit and thereafter with alternate units so as to prevent the precipitation of heart failure as a result of fluid overload.

Notes

1 When giving platelet transfusions it is worth remembering that whereas the platelets may be of a suitable group, they are rarely perfectly matched and thus transfusion reactions can still occur with the subsequent lysis of platelets. If your patient reacts to the transfusion or s/he is known to have had a reaction to previous transfusions give 100 mg of hydrocortisone and 10 mg of chlorpheniramine IV prior to the transfusion. If the patient has had a severe reaction in the past then HLA-matched platelets are available but should only be used if absolutely necessary.

2 Transplant recipients, neonates, patients undergoing open heart surgery and children with acute leukaemia who are CMV-antibody negative should be given blood products that are CMV-negative.

3 You cannot infuse dextrose and blood into the same line because red blood cell rouleaux formations will occur. Thus beware of infusing blood via a line already used for an infusion of a drug made up in dextrose. Flush with 10 ml of saline between use.

Emergency transfusions (see also under Gastrointestinal bleeding (Chapter 6))

If the situation is life-threatening then 'O' negative blood can be used before the cross-match is complete. Alternatively, colloids can be used whilst waiting for the blood to arrive.

It is worth remembering that if you are using copious quantities of packed cells, the remaining plasma, clotting factors and platelets will be diluted. As a rough guide use 2 u of fresh frozen plasma for every 4 u of packed cells to counteract this loss of clotting potential. Platelet transfusions for low platelets are rarely required unless the patient is actively bleeding. Remember also that you may need to replace calcium if the transfusion continues for a long period — 10 ml of 10% calcium gluconate for every 4–6 u.

Reactions

These may be mild or severe. A pyrexia is very common. If it is less than 39˚C and the patient is otherwise well then it will usually settle with 1 g of paracetamol po/pr and by slowing down the transfusion.

If it is more than 39˚C or the patient develops an urticarial rash with or without hypotension and with or without wheezing then you are dealing with a *blood transfusion reaction*. Proceed as follows:

1 Stop the transfusion and return the remainder to the laboratory.

2 Administer 10 mg chlorpheniramine and 200 mg hydrocortisone IV.

3 If the patient is unwell and deteriorating call for help. If the situation is life-threatening give: 0.5 ml of a 1 in 1000 solution of adrenaline IM.

4 Re-check both the patient's and the donor's blood for compatibility.

5 Watch out for the sudden development of ARF.

Headaches

Ninety per cent of the adult population will have a simple tension headache at some point in their lives and there is no reason at all why this can't occur in hospital. However, severe headaches with systemic symptoms should be taken seriously. The main diagnoses to consider are:

Migraine (the commonest cause)

These often follow a set pattern. A sense of ill health leads to a visual aura and then a throbbing headache (usually unilateral). It may be associated with anorexia, nausea, vomiting, photophobia and withdrawal. There may be transient hemiparesis or sensory symptoms.

Meningitis

Beware of a history of intense malaise, rigors, vomiting, severe headache, photophobia. Signs include pyrexia, neck stiffness, and a positive Kernig's sign.

Subarachnoid haemorrhage

Characterised by a sudden, severe occipital headache. It may be associated with nausea and vomiting, photophobia, neck stiffness and sometimes loss of consciousness.

Giant cell arteritis

Pain over the temples or over the entire scalp. Check the ESR urgently and consider giving steroids to protect the patient's sight.

Hypertensive encephalopathy

Usually associated with a diastolic BP of more than 140 mmHg although it can occur with a diastolic pressure as low as 100 mmHg. Characterised by headache, vomiting and deterioration in vision. Ophthalmoscopy reveals retinal haemorrhages and papilloedema. Urinalysis demonstrates proteinuria.

Subdural haematoma

Particularly likely in the elderly, in alcoholics or in children who have been involved in trauma. Characterised by increasing confusion, fluctuating level of consciousness and neurological symptoms and signs. There may well be signs of raised intracranial pressure (falling pulse rate, rising BP and papilloedema).

Most of the above require expert management once the diagnosis has been made, so contact your chiefs.

The acute red eye

If you are called to the ward to assess a patient with an 'acute red eye', your main objective is to rule out a diagnosis requiring urgent specialist treatment, i.e.:

- acute glaucoma
- acute iritis
- corneal ulceration.

In all cases:
- do a careful examination
- assess visual acuity
- assess the cornea
- assess pupillary reflexes.

If you are in doubt about any of the conditions listed in Table 6.6, ask for help.

Table 6.6 Major causes of an acute red eye

Acute glaucoma
Vision is reduced; pain is variable; hazy cornea as a result of oedema; circumcorneal redness; fixed, dilated, slightly ovoid pupil; hard eyeball

Acute iritis
Acute onset of pain; photophobia; blurred vision due to precipitates; lacrimation; circumcorneal redness; *small pupil;* later the pupil may become irregularly shaped

Corneal ulcers
Pain; photophobia; sometimes blurred vision. Diagnosis aided by 1% fluorescein drops — if there is an abrasion these will stain green

Conjunctivitis
Red and inflamed conjunctiva; vision, pupillary response and corneal lustre all normal; eye itchy, burning and watering; photophobia; purulent discharge

Subconjunctival haemorrhage
A spontaneous subconjunctival bleed occurring without history of trauma. You can see the posterior border

Fits

Treat calls such as this as an emergency. Invariably when you arrive the patient has stopped fitting because most fits self-terminate within 5 min. If so, no immediate treatment is required but it is vital to get an accurate description of the fit to rule out the possibility that you are dealing with something other than a fit — such as rigors.

A typical grand-mal fit follows the following pattern:

1 Rigid phase (tonic phase) — lasting up to a minute.

2 A convulsion (clonic phase) in which muscles jerk rhythmically — lasts for a few seconds to a few minutes.

3 Leaves the patient feeling drowsy or in a coma for up to several hours.

Should you arrive whilst the patient is still fitting or if the fits have followed one another (status epilepticus) there is a serious risk of death from cardiorespiratory failure. Thus immediate treatment is required. Your aim is to prevent the patient from coming to any harm (including the prevention of hypoxia).

1 Place the patient into the recovery position and if possible put in an airway — but *never* force one in.

2 Apply 100% oxygen through a mask — unless contra-indicated.

3 Establish venous access (often very difficult).

4 Give 10 mg Diazemuls IV stat or give rectal diazepam if IV access is not possible. (Just squeeze in via syringe without a needle!)

5 If unsuccessful call for help and ask somebody to look for some phenytoin. See under Drug infusions (Chapter 2).

Once the fit has terminated, look for a cause (Table 6.7). Always check the blood sugar by ward glucose assay and if the patient is hypoglycaemic give 50 ml of 50% glucose IV immediately. Check for a history of rising BP suggestive of rising intracranial pressure.

Discuss the need for long-term anti-epileptics.

It is important to remember that anyone who has suffered a fit is unable to drive a vehicle in the UK unless they have been free from any form of epileptic attack whilst awake for a period of 2 years or they have had fits confined to sleep for 3 years prior to the issue of a licence. Note also that anyone who has

Table 6.7 Major causes of grand mal fits

Idiopathic
Trauma and surgery
Cerebral infarction
Drugs, alcohol and drug withdrawal — including the accidental leaving-off of
    anti-epileptics from the drug chart
Encephalitis and other inflammatory conditions of the brain
Metabolic causes
    Hypocalcaemia
    Hypoglycaemia
    Hyponatraemia
    Acute hypoxia
    Porphyria
    Uraemia
    Hepatic failure

had a fit after the age of 3 years is banned from holding a public service or heavy goods vehicle licence for life.

The basic investigations are: U & E, glucose, calcium, arterial blood gas, with or without a CT scan.

Diabetes and ward glucose assays

A number of patients on the ward will regularly have their blood sugar tested with the use of ward glucose assay, e.g. BM Stix. You will be called to the ward on endless occasions if the readings are high or low. Always remember that this assay is only an approximation of the blood glucose level.

Low readings

Any patient with a ward glucose assay reading of less than 2.3 mmol/l should receive treatment before the laboratory blood glucose result is available.

MANAGEMENT
1 Take blood sample for laboratory blood glucose estimation.
2 If the patient is conscious, administer concentrated sugar in

the form of Lucozade, a glucose drink or sweet tea. If unconscious, give 50 ml of 50% dextrose IV stat.
3 Maintain hourly ward glucose recordings and keep the blood glucose between 5 and 12 mmol/l.

NB: It is often useful to prescribe glucagon 1 mg IM on the prn side of the drug chart for all insulin dependent diabetics, so that it may be given rapidly by the nursing staff during a hypoglycaemic emergency.

If the patient is repeatedly becoming hypoglycaemic then:
1 Investigate the cause — review the prescribed oral hypogly-caemics and insulins which may need altering in dose and timing.
2 Set up a 10% dextrose drip and keep it running for at least 48 h, particularly if the patient has been rendered hypoglyca-emic by long-acting insulins or has been overdosed on oral hypoglycaemics (Table 6.8).

High readings
Your main aim is to avoid diabetic keto-acidosis or non-ketotic diabetic coma and thus it is essential that you take these calls seriously. Should a non-fasting ward glucose reading be more than 11 mmol/l then it should be considered high (more than 7 mmol/l in a fasting patient). You must consider:
1 The accuracy of the ward assay — therefore check the level with a laboratory assay.
2 The timing of the assay in relation to the last meal.
3 The timing of the assay in relation to the dose and type of insulin or oral hypoglycaemic.
4 The absence or presence of ketones in the urine.

Remember that the peak glucose blood level after a meal is approximately 2 h. The duration of action of insulins and oral hypoglycaemics is shown in Table 6.8.

Table 6.8 Insulins and oral hypoglycaemics — onset, peak and duration of action

	Onset	Peak	Duration
SC insulins			
Short acting	30–60 min	2–4 h	up to 8 h
Intermediate acting	1–2 h	4–12 h	16–35 h
IV insulins			
Short acting	5 min	10–15 min	30 min
Oral hypoglycaemics			
Tolbutamide	3–4 h	7 h	12 h
Chlorpropamide	1–7 h	8–12 h	33–43 h

Examples of insulins:
- Short acting: Velosulin, Actrapid, Humulin
- Intermediate acting: Insulatard
- Long acting: Monotard, Lentard
- Biphasic insulins: Mixtard or Humulin M (30% short acting and 70% intermediate acting).

If you are called to see a diabetic patient with a raised blood sugar and negative urinary ketones who is on bd insulin or oral hypoglycaemics then:

1 Assess whether the general control is poor by looking at the previous 48 h ward glucose recordings.

2 If the control is poor then you should consider increasing the doses of either the insulin (by no more than a couple of units) or the oral hypoglycaemic (Table 6.9).

3 If the control is generally good and this is an abnormally high reading for the patient, you must:

    (a) test the blood sugar in the laboratory, and

    (b) if this confirms that the result is high, seek a cause. It is most likely to be dietary (such as a sugary meal or drink prior to the test) but may have been precipitated by the presence of infection or other cause of catecholamine output.

NB: If the patient has asymptomatic hyperglycaemia, there is no place for stat doses of insulin since diabetic keto-acidosis

Table 6.9 A guide to the modification of a twice daily (short and intermediate acting) insulin regimen

	Fasting (mane)	Before lunch	Before evening meal	Bedtime
Persistent hyperglycaemia (BM > 10 mmol/l)	↑evening intermediate acting 2–4 u	↑morning short acting 2–4 u or ↓breakfast or mid-morning snack	↑morning intermediate acting 2–4 u or ↓afternoon snack	↑evening short acting 2–4 u or ↓evening snack
Persistent hypoglycaemia (symptomatic or BM < 4 mmol/l)	↓evening intermediate acting 2–4 u	↓morning short acting 2–4 u or ↑mid-morning carbohydrate	↓morning intermediate acting 2–4 u or ↑afternoon carbohydrate	↓evening short acting 2–4 u or ↑evening meal carbohydrate

Reproduced with permission of Weatherall, D.J., Ledingham, J.G.G. and Warrell, D.A. (1987) *Oxford Textbook of Medicine* Second edn, Oxford University Press.

takes days rather than hours to develop. If however the patient is symptomatic (polyuria, polydipsia) and has ketones in the urine then you must obtain:

1 Arterial blood gas estimation.
2 Blood sugar.
3 U & E.

If the patient is acidotic then s/he has a diabetic keto-acidosis. Treat with fluid replacement and insulin infusions — see under Drug infusions (Chapter 2).

Diagnosis of diabetes

Most of the time the diagnosis of diabetes mellitus is easily made on the basis of a history of weight loss associated with polydipsia, polyuria and the finding of a raised blood glucose level (for normal values see under Chemical pathology tests in Chapter 7). The situation is more difficult in the case of an asymptomatic patient.

The World Health Organisation has produced criteria for the diagnosis of diabetes (revised 1985) but the issue of whether a diagnosis of diabetes in an asymptomatic patient should be made on the basis of a single abnormal result is still disputed. The consensus of opinion would appear to suggest that two abnormal readings are necessary and these abnormal results must not be due to an obvious hyperglycaemic stimulus such as high-dose steroids. If the situation is not clear, two further measures may be employed:

1 Assay of fasting glucose levels.

2 An oral glucose tolerance test (this should be reserved for truly borderline cases) — see Chapter 7 for protocol.

NOTES

1 Find out whether your laboratory results refer to plasma glucose levels or whole blood glucose levels. The normal ranges are different and this is an important distinction.

2 There may be a transient increase in the blood sugar in ill patients due to the excess catecholamines in the blood. Re-check the blood glucose at a later date.

3 If a patient has abnormal blood glucose results due to one of the many groups of drugs that impair glucose metabolism (e.g. diuretics), this dose not equate with a diagnosis of diabetes.

4 Glycosuria likewise does not necessarily equate with diabetes since the patient's renal threshold for glucose may be low. In any patient with glycosuria it is essential to check a random blood glucose.

The confused patient

It is amazing how many people suffer acute confusional states whilst in hospital. In particular you will be faced with several patients who return from the operating theatre apparently 'mad': disoriented, kicking, screaming and pulling out every tube in sight. They can make both medical and nursing management very difficult and are at risk of causing themselves harm.

You *must* try to look for a treatable cause of this apparent madness (Table 6.10). Very often, however, you will find no clear cause especially in the elderly who can become confused simply by the change in environment imposed upon them by coming into hospital. You should try to obtain as full a history as possible (often not available from the patient), perform an examination, and do appropriate investigations as required. It may be useful to get an idea of the pre-morbid personality from close friends or relatives.

Table 6.10   Major causes of confusion

Hypoxia
Pain or discomfort (e.g. urinary retention)
Alcohol withdrawal (very common)
Hypokalaemia
Infection
Hypo/hyperglycaemia
Hypo/hypernatraemia
Hypo/hypercalcaemia

All the causes may be exacerbated by anaemia, hypotension or pre-existing dementia. *Never* attempt to sedate an uncontrollable patient without due consideration of the cause since it may make the situation worse and could even be fatal. If sedation is vital or deemed unharmful you can give one of the following:
• Chlorpromazine: 25–50 mg every 6–8 h.
• Chlormethiazole: oral or IV (see Chapter 2).
• Haloperidol: up to 30 mg IM, then 5 mg every hour as necessary.
• Diazepam: 10 mg IV over 2 min (or give rectally). Repeat if necessary after 4 h.
• Lorazepam: up to 2 mg IV slowly.

PRACTICAL TIPS
1 Be cautious about the use of cot sides. A confused mobile patient may well climb over them and cause themselves a

worse injury by way of the distance they have fallen. Many wards now place the patient on a mattress on the floor to avoid this problem of falling out of bed — and the need to fill in the ensuing Accident Form.

2 If you want IV lines to remain in place you should stick them down with the stickiest tape available to you and ask the nursing staff to bandage the arm. You could also put mittens on the patient's hand if warranted.

3 No matter how frustrated you may become with these patients, *never* use force.

4 Try keeping a night light on by the elderly confused patient, since darkness exacerbates their confusion.

The moribund patient

We can guarantee that you will at some stage be asked to see a patient who has suddenly become unwell and about whom the staff is severely worried. It is often difficult not to develop the same degree of panic that may be developing on the ward and to feel overwhelmed by the ongoing situation. Whatever you do, *don't panic*. It is imperative that you think quickly but logically about what might be going on, but above all stay calm: if you don't, nobody else will.

Obtain a quick assessment of the patient's history and progress while s/he has been in hospital, if the patient is not known to you. Perform a basic but thorough examination. Gain IV access and send off appropriate blood samples. Do an ECG, a portable CXR, and arterial blood gas, U & E, FBC etc., as time permits. Check the resuscitation status of the patient and call for help if you feel that you are out of your depth.

We have presented here a list of possible causes for this worrying clinical situation (Table 6.11). This might seem a little obvious but often half of your feelings of dread result from the fact that under pressure your mind goes blank and you cannot even begin to interpret the situation.

Table 6.11 Conditions to look for in the acutely unwell patient

- Acute LVF
- Cardiogenic shock
- CVA
- Dissecting aortic aneurysm
- Encephalopathy: hypertensive, hepatic, renal, Wernicke's
- Hypoglycaemia
- Hypothermia
- Hypovolaemia (e.g. acute haemorrhage)
- MI or dysrhythmia
- Narcotic overdose — particularly postoperatively
- PE
- Perforated viscus
- Pneumonia
- Post-ictal
- Sepsis leading to shock

Rashes

'Mrs A has a funny rash.'

When this call arrives you will wish you had been a keener dermatology student! A great many rashes which develop whilst in hospital are drug-related. The list of possible diagnoses is enormous but it is often a good idea to start by looking through the patient's drug chart to try to isolate a cause.

Urticaria: with penicillins and cephalosporins this commonly occurs 3–7 days after therapy has commenced — but can begin at any time.

Purpura: this may be a feature of any severe drug reaction or septicaemia and results from capillary damage.

Consider also:
- light-sensitive reactions
- fixed drug reactions
- eczema
- psoriasis

- herpes zoster

Essentially, if the patient is systemically well and if nobody is available for a second opinion and the patient is itching, treat symptomatically. If you feel an antihistamine is warranted, choose the specific drug after consideration as to whether or not sedation would be an advantage:

- Sedating antihistamines: chlorpheniramine 4 mg tds.
- Non-sedating: terfenadine 60 mg bd.

Also prescribe cooling lotions as required (e.g. calamine) unless you want a dermatologist to see the patient.

If the patient is pyrexial — call for help as many serious bacterial infections are associated with rashes and pyrexias and need appropriate management quickly.

Perform basic blood tests including a clotting screen.

7: The Medical Laboratory

The number of tests you will be asked to perform is daunting. Although you will rapidly become familiar with the procedure for performing the most regular, there will be others you know little about. Most frustratingly, you may be unsure which tube the blood needs to go in and what the significance of the result is when it finally comes back.

To find out more, you will have to contact the relevant laboratory but invariably their phone will be engaged, and what seems like a simple task will rapidly turn into a time-consuming saga.

Hence we have included this chapter, which we hope will explain how to perform the majority of blood tests. We have also included brief comments on the results so that you can report any abnormalities to your seniors with an iota of understanding which otherwise might not have been present!

The data given in the tables in this chapter are compiled from several sources including Birch, C.A., Surtrees, S.J. and Wray, R. (1980) *The House Physician's Handbook*, Fifth edn, Churchill Livingstone, Edinburgh.

Which tube for which test? (Table 7.1)
There are two main colour-coding systems in operation in the UK: the Vacutainer system and a non-evacuated system.

High-risk samples
It is in everyone's interests that you follow the basic 'high-risk' policies that exist in your hospital because you will be held accountable for the consequences of someone becoming infected with HIV or hepatitis B, for example, if you fail to undertake suitable precautions. These precautions include:

1 Clear labelling of high-risk samples: some hospitals have a specific colour coding system for samples which may be HIV positive.

Table 7.1 Main colour-coding systems for tubes.

Sample type	Uses	Colour	
		Vacutainer	Non-evacuated
EDTA	FBC, sickle test, Hb, Hb electrophoresis, G6PD enzyme assay, malaria etc.	Purple	Pink
Citrate 1 : 9	Coagulation tests, PT, PTTK, INR etc.	Blue	Mauve
Citrate 1 : 4	ESR	Black	Blue
Fluoride/oxalate	Plasma glucose/ alcohol	Grey	Yellow
Lithium heparin[b]	Chromosome analysis	Green	Orange
Plain/clotted	Microbiology, serology, general chemistry, drugs	Mottled top or red or brown[a]	White
	Transfusion sample – G & S or CM	Pink	Red

[a] The mottled-top tube contains a serum separation gel which reduces the chance of haemolysis.

[b] Many laboratories prefer to use a lithium heparin tube for many tests because it is easier to handle.

Some laboratories use a special tube for cardiac enzymes or metals.

Hb = haemoglobin; G6PD = glucose-6-phosphate dehydrogenase.

Samples key:

A = arterial heparinised sample

C = clotted

CSF = cerebrospinal fluid

EDTA = ethylene diamine tetra-acetic acid

F = fluoride

H = heparin lithium

MSU = mid-stream sample of urine

R = random urine sample

Sp. = special — contact the relevant laboratory

24 h = 24 h urine collection

2 You may be required to place high-risk samples into two specimen bags.

It may take a little longer to do various tests on high-risk patients but this time is obviously well spent. High-risk patients are those suspected or known to be:

1 IV drug abusers.

2 Homosexual/bisexual.

3 Patients with HIV infection or carriage.

4 Patients with hepatitis B infection or carriage.

5 Patients from sub-Saharan Africa.

6 Haemophiliacs.

7 Sexual partners of any of the above.

Haematology tests

Test	Sample	Reference value	Comments
Activated partial thromboplastin time (APTT) (= KCCT)	Citrate	30–40 s	Measures the intrinsic system: factors VIII, IX, XI & XII, in addition to factors common to both
Antithrombin III	Citrate	Percentage of normal	A potent inhibitor of thrombin, potentiated by heparin. Thus check levels before giving heparin. A reduction of levels below about 60% leads to a thrombotic tendency
Bleeding time	—	1–7 min	Raised in aspirin therapy and thrombocytopenia. A test of platelet function
Blood count			See haemoglobin, leucocytes, MCH, red cell(s), reticulocytes and platelets
Clotting factors:	Citrate		
XIII — fibrin stabilising factor		10 mg/l	
XII — Hageman factor		40 mg/l	
XI — plasma thromboplastin antecedent		5 mg/l	
X — *Stuart Prower factor		10 mg/l	
IX — *Christmas factor		5–10 mg/l	
VIII — antihaemophilic factor		200 µg/l	
VII — *proconvertin		500 µg/l	
V — labile factor		10 mg/l	
II — *prothrombin		100 mg/l	
I — fibrinogen		2–4 g/l	
Protein C — autoprothrombin		5 mg/l ⎫	Low levels may produce a thrombotic tendency, so always check before commencing anticoagulants
*Protein S — II A		20 mg/l ⎭	
Coombs' test	C	—	*Direct*: indicates whether RBCs are coated with antibody — as in haemolytic disease of the new born. *Indirect*: indicates presence of antibody to RBCs in patient sera

Haematology tests (*continued*)

Test	Sample	Reference value	Comments
Cryoglobulins	C		Serum proteins which precipitate at < 37°C *Type 1*: monoclonal immunoglobulin of Bence-Jones proteinuria *Type 2*: mixed form with a monoclonal component acting as an antibody against polyclonal IgG *Type 3*: mixed form with one or more classes of polyclonal IgG
D dimers	Citrate		See FDPs
Erythrocytes	EDTA		See red cell count
ESR	Citrate	Male: 0–8 mm/h Female: 0–12 mm/h Elderly: < 30 mm/h	Raised in pregnancy, most infections and inflammations Very high (>100 mm/h) in TB, multiple myeloma, renal carcinoma, temporal arteritis
Factor VIII	Citrate	Percentage of normal	< 1% = severe haemophilia 1–5% = moderate haemophilia 5–20% = mild haemophilia
Ferritin	C	20–200 µg/l	Low in iron deficiency. High in haemachromatosis, overtransfusion, chronic liver disease
FDPs	Sp.	Check with laboratory	Very high (> 40) in DIC. High in DVT, liver disease, bacterial infection. D dimers are a more specific assessment of clotting activity
Fibrinogen	Citrate	2-4 g/l	Low in DIC. High in PE and nephrotic syndrome
Folate (serum)	C	5–60 nmol/l (3–15 µg/l)	Reflects folate absorption in the past few weeks (see also red cell folate)
G-6-P dehydrogenase enzyme assay	EDTA	Check with laboratory	Must be done when patient is not actively haemolysing since this will increase the reticulocytes and hence give a falsely raised enzyme level

Haematology tests (*continued*)

Test	Sample	Reference value	Comments
Haematocrit	EDTA		See PCV
Hb	EDTA	Male: 13–18 g/dl Female: 11.5–16.5 g/dl	
Hb electrophoresis	EDTA		Normal Hb in adult blood: HbA (α2, β2) — 96–98% HbA$_2$ (α2, δ2) — 1.5–3.2% HbF (α2, γ2) — 0.5–0.8%
HbA$_1$ C (glycosylated Hb)	EDTA	3–7%	Higher level indicates poor diabetic control
HbS	EDTA		Abnormal Hb present in sickle cells. Sickle cell disease: HbA — nil HbF — 5–15% HbS — 85–95% Sickle cell trait: HbS — 25–45%
Haptoglobins	C	20–125 μmol/l (0.3–2.0 g/l)	An alpha-2 globulin. Reduced in haemolytic anaemias. Raised in pregnancy, chronic infection and steroid therapy
Iron	C	Male: 14–32 μmol/l Female: 11–30 μmol/l	Decreased in iron deficiency anaemia. Increased in haemochromatosis. See also ferritin and TIBC
INR			See PT
KCCT			See PTT

Haematology tests (*continued*)

Test	Sample	Reference value	Comments
Leucocytes	EDTA	$4-11 \times 10^9/l$	Surprisingly high WCC can result from vigorous exercise including a grand-mal fit. A leucocytosis may also be found in pregnancy. Neutrophil count $2.0-7.5 \times 10^9/l$ = 40–75% WCC Lymphocytes $1.5-3.5 \times 10^9/l$ = 20–45% WCC Eosinophils $0.04-0.44 \times 10^9/1$ = 1–6% WCC Basophils $0-0.1 \times 10^9/l$ = 0.2–0.8% WCC Monocytes $0.2-0.8 \times 10^9/l$ = 2–10% WCC
Malaria	EDTA		Three negative samples are required to refute the diagnosis
MCH	EDTA	27–32 pg	Decreased in iron deficiency anaemia
MCHC	EDTA	30–36 g/dl	Decreased in iron deficiency anaemia
MCV	EDTA	75–95 fl	If >95 fl, indicates macrocytosis. Many causes including B_{12} or folate deficiency, alcohol abuse, liver disease, many drugs, reticulocytosis. If <75 fl, indicates microcytosis. Most common cause is iron deficiency anaemia
Methaemalbumin	C	Negative	An indication of intravascular haemolysis
Methaemoglobin	H	0.5–3.0%	Represents Hb in which haem is in the ferric form. Useless as an oxygen carrier. May be a congenital or acquired condition (e.g. drugs — quinones, ferricyanide). May be chronic or acute. Up to 10–20% tolerated quite well
Neutrophil alkaline phosphatase score	Sp.	10–100 per 100 neutrophils	Elevated in infection, inflammation, tissue necrosis. Subnormal in CML, PNH. Contact laboratory first

Haematology tests (*continued*)

Test	Sample	Reference value	Comments
Osmotic fragility	H	0.4–0.45 g/dl of saline	Haemolytic anaemias are associated with increased red cell fragility
PCV	EDTA	Male: 0.4–0.54 = 40–54% Female: 0.37–0.47 = 37–47%	Raised in polycythaemia. Related to blood volume. Often a better guide to transfusion requirements than Hb
PTT, PTTK	Citrate	22–38 s	Compare with control. A test for factor VIII and prolonged in factor I, II, V, IX, XI, XII deficiency
Paul–Bunnell	C		Usually positive at some stage of glandular fever
Platelets	EDTA	150–400 × 10^9/l	Risk of bleeding is considerable if the level is below 20×10^9/l. Levels raised after surgery, chronic bleeding, polycythaemia rubra vera and active inflammation
PT	Citrate	11–14 s	Ensure an accurate amount of blood is sent for assay. The INR represents the ratio of the patient's PT to a standard control. See Oral anticoagulation therapy, Chapter 2
Red cell count	EDTA	Male: $4.5–6.0 \times 10^{12}$/l Female: $4.2–5.5 \times 10^{12}$/l	
Red cell folate	EDTA	160–640 g/l 0.36–1.44 μmol/l	More accurate than serum folate as a guide to tissue folate status
Red cell fragility	H		See osmotic fragility

Haematology tests (*continued*)

Test	Sample	Reference value	Comments
Reticulocytes	EDTA	0.2–2.0%	Raised in haemolytic anaemia, after haemorrhage and during treatment of anaemia. Reticulocyte count begins to rise 48 h after treatment for pernicious anaemia: peaks in 5–7 days
Sickle cell screen	EDTA		Sickle positive if cells sickle when the blood is deoxygenated with dithionate and Na_2HPO_4. Trait and disease differentiated by electrophoresis
Thalassaemia			Request Hb electrophoresis to show abnormal proportions of HbA_2 and HbA.
Thrombin time	Citrate	*c*.5 s	Compare with control. A test for fibrinogen (factor I)
TIBC	C	50–75 µmol/l	Increased in iron deficiency anaemia. Decreased in chronic inflammatory conditions and haemochromatosis
Vitamin B_{12}	C	0.13–0.68 nmol/l	Reduced in pernicious anaemia, patients with an ileal resection or malabsorption. Raised in myeloproliferative disorders and liver disease

* Vitamin K dependent factors.
Clotting factor details reproduced with permission of Weatherall, D.J., Ledingham, J.G.G. and Warrel, D.A. (1987) *Oxford Textbook of Medicine*, Second edn, Oxford University Press.
For key to samples, see footnote to Table 7.1.

Chemical pathology tests

Test	Sample	Reference value	Comments
ALT	H	5–35 iu/l	Avoid haemolysis. Levels raised in necrosis of liver or heart cells
Albumin	H	35–45 g/l	Low in chronic liver disease, malabsorption states, enteropathy and nephrotic syndrome
Alcohol (ethanol)	F	Legal limit: 80 mg/dl (17.4 mmol/l)	Do not use alcohol skin swab. Fatal level 500 mg/dl. Must fill bottle to top
Aldolase	C	1–8 iu/l	Raised in MI, muscular dystrophies, haemolytic anaemia, metastatic carcinoma of prostate, leukaemia, acute pancreatitis, hepatitis. Destruction of tissue results in release of aldolase into serum
ALP	H	Total 30–300 iu/l Leucocyte 25–100 iu/l	Levels may be more than double in children. Also raised in pregnancy, bone disease, biliary obstruction and primary hyperparathyroidism with associated bone disease. Decreased in hypophosphataemia. Avoid haemolysis. Leucocyte ALP — raised in leucocytosis. Reduced in myeloid leukaemia. Check result against age-adjusted range
Alpha-1-antitrypsin	C	1–5 g/l	Acute phase protein so assay performed when patient not otherwise unwell. High in cirrhosis, cholestasis, infections. Low in hepatic cirrhosis, severe protein deficiency, congenital. If low, then send off for genotype, e.g. MZ or ZZ in emphysematous patients
Alpha fetoprotein	C	Check with laboratory	Raised in teratoma (see under Oncology tests). Low in Down's syndrome, neural tube defects

Chemical pathology tests (*continued*)

Test	Sample	Reference value	Comments
Aluminium	C/Sp.	0.07–0.55 μmol/l	High in renal failure, dialysis encephalopathy, medication. Beware of contamination
Ammonia	Sp.	14–45 μmol/l	Arrange with laboratory first. Take sample after high protein meal if not contra-indicated. Deliver sample to laboratory immediately. Levels raised in hepatic insufficiency
Amylase	H	< 180 iu/l	May be raised in mumps, peptic ulceration, dissecting aortic aneurysm. Usually >1000 in acute pancreatitis. Unhelpful in chronic pancreatitis
Angiotensin converting enzyme	H	Check with laboratory	May be raised in sarcoidosis, lymphoma, TB, asbestosis and silicosis. Of use in assessing disease activity in sarcoidosis
Angiotensin II	H	5–35 pmol/l	Collect in heparin at mid-morning. Unstable hormone requiring immediate blood separation. Patient must rest 12 h before test, and be off all drugs for 1 month
Anion gap			See under Biochemical equations
Ascorbate	H	35–80 μmol/l	Levels reflect turnover. Low in scurvy, rickets. Saturation test more useful i.e. load and measure in urine
AST	C	5–35 iu/l	Avoid haemolysis. Levels raised within 6–18 h of an MI, peak at 1–2 days, normal at day 5. Also raised in hepatic necrosis, PE, alcohol excess
Base excess	H	– 2 to + 2 mmol/l	See Arterial blood gas estimation (Chapter 3)
Beta-carotene	H	1.0–5.6 μmol/l	Decreased in malabsorption

Chemical pathology tests (*continued*)

Test	Sample	Reference value	Comments
Beta-2-microglobulin	C	1.1–2.4 mg/l	Acute phase protein useful as a marker in multiple myeloma
Bicarbonate (total)	C	21–31 mmol/l	Raised in COAD, low in acidosis
Bicarbonate (standard)	H	21–36 mmol/l	See under Arterial blood gas estimation, Chapter 3
Bilirubin	H	Total < 19 μmol/l Direct < 7 μmol/l	Avoid haemolysis. Classically, unconjugated fraction raised in haemolytic anaemia, and conjugated fraction raised in hepatocellular disease and cholestasis — however, only rarely need to know the split
Blood gas determination	A		For method, normal values and interpretation see under Arterial blood gas estimation (Chapter 3)
Cadmium	H	1.8–2.7 μg/l (27–480 nmol/l)	Higher in smokers — 24 h urine screen available
Caeruloplasmin	C	0.2–0.5 g/l	An alpha-2 globulin. Contains most of the serum copper. Decreased in Wilson's disease and nephrosis. Raised in pregnancy
Calcium	H	2.20–2.60 mmol/l	Preferably assay blood in the fasted state. Avoid using a tourniquet. See under Biochemical equations for correction if albumin abnormal. Raised in malignancy, sarcoidosis, primary hyperparathyroidism, hypervitaminosis D, neonates, milk-alkali syndrome, myelomatosis. Reduced in hypoparathyroidism or pseudohypoparathyroidism, malabsorption, renal disease, osteomalacia, pancreatitis
Carboxyhaemo-globin	H	< 0.03 (3%)	May be raised in heavy smokers. Coma at 50%; 70% and over usually fatal

Chemical pathology tests (*continued*)

Test	Sample	Reference value	Comments
Chloride	H	95–105 mmol/l	High in hyperchloraemic acidosis after uterocolic implantation, RTA. Low in dehydration, diuretics, alcoholism, chronic or severe diarrhoea
Cholesterol	C	3.0–7.5 mmol/l <5.2 desirable	Assay after 14 h fast and 72 h abstinence from alcohol. Falsely high values after MI. Raised in cholestasis, nephrosis, type II & III hyperlipidaemia
Cholinesterase	H	2.25–7.0 iu/l	Decreased in organophosphorus poisoning. Genetic variants have reduced activity and may have extreme sensitivity to suxamethonium
Chromium	C	94–180 nmol/l	
Copper	H	13–24 μmol/l	Reduced in late-stage hepatolenticular degeneration (Wilson's disease). High in anaemia, infection, cirrhosis, hepatoma
Coproporphyrins	H	0–60 nmol/l	Increased in congenital porphyria and lead poisoning
C-reactive protein	C	< 8 mg/l	An acute-phase protein
CK, CPK	H	Male: 25–210 iu/l Female: 25–190 iu/l	Avoid haemolysis. Raised within 4 h of MI returning to normal in 3 days. If the maximum level reached is very high this indicates an extensive infarct. Also raised in any disease involving muscle damage including muscular dystrophy, IM injection and exercise (including CPR)
CK-MB	H	0–8 iu/l	Cardiac specific isoenzyme of CK. Rises within 4 h of MI, peaking at about 24 h and returning to normal after about 48 h

Chemical pathology tests (*continued*)

Test	Sample	Reference value	Comments
Creatinine	H	60–130 µmol/l	Avoid haemolysis. Lipaemia also interferes with assay. Raised in renal failure. Unlike urea not greatly affected by dietary factors
Creatinine clearance	C/U	90–120 ml/min	24 h urine collection also required — see under Urine assays. Must measure plasma creatinine during the same 24 h period as the urine collection
Fructosamine	C	1.8–2.7 mmol/l	Avoid haemolysis
Gamma-GT	H	Male: 11–63 iu/l Female: 8–35 iu/l	Avoid haemolysis. Levels parallel alkaline phosphatase in cholestasis but often rises earlier. Not altered by bone disease. Raised after alcohol intake
Gastrin	H	< 40 pmol/l	Arrange with laboratory first. Need serum calcium and urea results. Transfer to laboratory immediately on ice. Raised in Zollinger–Ellison syndrome

Globulin fractions
    alpha-1
    alpha-2
    beta
    gamma
    beta-1
    transferrin
	C	
		2–4 g/l
		5–9 g/l
		6–11 g/l
		7–17 g/l
		1.2–2.0 g/l	

Glucose Fasting	F	Blood: 3.3–6.7 mmol/l Plasma: 4.1–7.8 mmol/l	These values are those set out in the WHO criteria for diagnosing diabetes. A fasting blood glucose result between 6.7 and 10 mmol/l should be followed by a glucose tolerance test. See under Dynamic tests
Random	F	Blood: 3.3–10 mmol/l Plasma: 4.1–11.1 mmol/l	

Chemical pathology tests (*continued*)

Test	Sample	Reference value	Comments
HDL cholesterol	C	1.0–1.5 mmol/l	Ratio of total cholesterol : HDL cholesterol is the best prognostic marker; it should not exceed 4.5. The higher the ratio the worse the prognosis
HBD	H	40–150 iu/l	Avoid haemolysis. This is an isoenzyme of LDH which is more cardiac specific. Levels reach peak at 48–72 h after MI, returning to normal after 7–10 days. Also raised in PE and in megaloblastic anaemia
Immunoglobulins	C		
IgG		7.2–19 g/l	
IgA		0.8–5.0 g/l	
IgM		0.5–2.0 g/l	
Lactate	Sp.	0.4–2 mmol/l	Arrange with laboratory first. Avoid stasis. Transfer to laboratory immediately. High in exercise, tissue hypoxia. Measured in anion gap
LDH	H	60–250 iu/l	Raised in PE, MI, megaloblastic anaemia, haemolytic anaemia, liver disease and muscular dystrophy
Lead	C	< 2 μmol/l	
Lipase	C	0.2–1.5 iu/l Method dependent	High in acute pancreatitis, Pancreatic duct obstruction
Lipoproteins	C		
VLDL		0.128–0.645 mmol/l	
LDL		1.55–4.4 mmol/l	
HDL		Male: 0.7–2.1 mmol/l Female: 0.50–1.70 mmol/l	

Chemical pathology tests (*continued*)

Test	Sample	Reference value	Comments
Magnesium	H	0.8–1.2 mmol/l (1.8–2.4 mg/ 100 ml)	Avoid haemolysis. Reduced levels in malabsorption and after prolonged IV therapy. Deficiency may cause tetany. Levels raised in renal failure, reduced in cisplatin tubular damage
Manganese	H	0.1–0.2 μmol/l	
5′-Nucleotidase	C	2–17 pmol/l	A liver enzyme sometimes used to confirm the hepatic origin of a raised alkaline phosphatase
Osmolality	C	275–305 mosmol/kg	Avoid haemolysis. High in hyperglycaemia, uraemia, DI, dehydration, alcohol abuse, true hypernatraemia. Low in hyponatraemia, water overload, inappropriate ADH secretion
Paraprotein	C/Sp.	Check with laboratory	Both serum and urine are essential for this test
Phosphate (inorganic)	H	0.75–1.4 mmol/l	Avoid haemolysis. Raised in renal failure, hypoparathyroidism, acromegaly. Reduced in hyperparathyroidism. Levels show a diurnal variation. Check age-adjusted reference range
Phospholipid	H	2.9–5.3 mmol/l	
Potassium	H	3.5–5.0 mmol/l	Avoid haemolysis
Protein (total)	H	62–82 g/l	Low in nephrotic syndrome, CRF, malnutrition. High in alcoholism, dehydration, multiple myeloma, lymphoma, auto-immune disease, chronic infection, prolonged tourniquet during venepuncture
Pyruvate	Sp.	40–70 μmol/l	Avoid venous stasis and transfer to laboratory immediately. High in thiamine deficiency

Chemical pathology tests (*continued*)

Test	Sample	Reference value	Comments
Sodium	H	135–145 mmol/l	Raised in water deprivation and DI. Low in diarrhoea, vomiting, diabetic coma, steroid deficiency, inappropriate ADH secretion, congenital adrenal hyperplasia, chronic alcoholism, Addison's disease
Transketolase (erythrocyte)	Sp.	Check with laboratory	In thiamine deficiency shows reduced activity, become normal after the addition of the cofactor thiamine pyrophosphate
Triglyceride	C	0.2–1.9 mmol/l	Assay after 14 h fast
Urate	H	Male: 0.2–0.45 mmol/l Female: 0.14–0.38 mmol/l	Female levels rise to male levels after menopause. Raised in gout, leukaemia, treatment of myeloproliferative disorders, renal failure
Urea	H	2.5–7.0 mmol/l	Levels reduced in pregnancy, childhood, liver disease. High in old age, renal failure, after GI bleed
Vitamin A	H	0.7–1.7 µmol/l	Sample should be kept in the dark to prevent destruction by ultraviolet light
Vitamin B$_1$	H	> 40 nmol/l	Low in beri-beri, Wernicke's encephalopathy
Vitamin B$_{12}$			See under Haematology tests
Vitamin D	C	Season-dependent	Low in rickets, stunted growth, tetany, osteomalacia. High in metastatic calcification with excess intake of calcium or its mobilisation from bone
Vitamin E	H	11–55 µmol/l	
Xylose	F	7.7–16 mmol/l	See under Xylose absorption tests

Chemical pathology tests (*continued*)

Test	Sample	Reference value	Comments
Zinc	Sp.	7–20 µmol/l	Low in cirrhosis, diarrhoea, malabsorption, alcoholism, drugs (steroids and diuretics). High in zinc therapy

For key to samples, see footnote to Table 7.1.

Endocrinology tests

Test	Sample	Reference value	Comments
ACTH	H	10–80 ng/l	Take blood between 0900 h and 1000 h. Contact laboratory; blood requires immediate separation
Adrenaline	Citrate	Check with your laboratory	Arrange with laboratory first
Aldosterone	H	100–400 pmol/l	May be useful in the investigation of Conn's syndrome and secondary aldosteronism but only indicated if patient is hypertensive and hypokalaemic. *Stop* diuretics and purgatives for 3 weeks beforehand. Take sample in the morning after rest. Take serum for sodium and potassium at the same time. Results are affected by posture
Androstenedione	C	Male: 1.2–8.6 nmol/l Female: 2–12 nmol/l	Female values reduce to male values after the menopause
ADH	H	1–4.5 pmol/l	
Calcitonin	H	< 27 pmol/l	Contact laboratory first. Transfer to laboratory on ice
Cortisol	H	At 2400 h 150–220 nmol/l At 0900 h 170–650 nmol/l	Random figures of no clinical significance
DHA sulphate	H	Male: < 5.6 nmol/l Female: 0.7–11.5 nmol/l	Female values fall to male values after the menopause
FSH	C	2–8 iu/l	Must indicate LMP on request form. Raised after menopause
Glucagon	H	< 50 pmol/l	Arrange with laboratory first
Gonadotrophins			See beta-HCG, FSH, LH

Endocrinology tests (*continued*)

Test	Sample	Reference value	Comments
Growth hormone	C	< 20 mU/l	See under Adrenopituitary function tests
Beta-HCG	C	< 5 iu/l	See under Oncology tests
Insulin	C	5–30 mU/l	Avoid haemolysis. Transfer to laboratory immediately. Take after overnight fast. Assay blood glucose simultaneously
Insulin C-peptide	C	0.5–2.5 µg/l	Not metabolised in the liver so more useful than insulin measurement as an assessment of endogenous insulin secretion. Also useful if you wish to assess the endogenous insulin production in an insulin-dependent diabetic whose administered insulin would interfere with the test
LH	C	6–13 iu/l	In females, range varies with stage of menstrual cycle. Levels raised in ovarian or testicular failure
Neurotensin	C	< 100 pmol/l	
Oestradiol (17β)	C	Male: < 200 pmol/l Female: Mid-cycle 700–1800 pmol/l Follicular 70–360 pmol/l Luteal 360–1100 pmol/l Postmenopausal < 185 pmol/l	Indicate LMP. Results may be used to monitor response of reproductive function or diagnosis of oestrogen producing tumours. Need sex hormone binding globulin level
Pancreatic polypeptide	Sp.	< 200 pmol/l	
PTH	C	0.1–0.73 µg/l	Patient must be fasted for 16 h. Assay calcium and urea simultaneously. Transfer to laboratory immediately

Endocrinology tests (*continued*)

Test	Sample	Reference value	Comments
Progesterone	H	Follicular <12 nmol/l Luteal >30 nmol/l	Indicate LMP on request form as levels vary with menstrual cycle. Absence of a mid-cycle rise suggests an anovulatory cycle. Levels raised in pregnancy
Prolactin	C	0–480 mU/l	May be of value in investigating pituitary tumours and in following up hypophysectomy patients. Hyperprolactinaemia is associated with amenorrhoea and infertility in women. Also may be associated with impotence in men. Avoid concurrent use of metoclopramide, haloperidol, tricyclic antidepressants, and other dopamine antagonists
Renin	H	Check with laboratory	Arrange with laboratory first. See aldosterone
Somatostatin	C	< 100 pmol/l	
Testosterone	C	Male: 10–30 nmol/l Female: 0.9–2.7 nmol/l	Need sex hormone binding globulin level
TBG	C	7–17 mg/l	Levels raised in pregnancy and on oestrogen therapy. Low in nephrosis
Thyroid function Total T4 Free T4 T3 Free T3 TSH	C	60–145 nmol/l 8.8–23 pmol/l 1.23–3 nmol/l 2.9–8.9 pmol/l 1.0–6.0 mU/l	If there is clear clinical suspicion of thyroid abnormality, give as much detail as possible on the request form (see under Dynamic tests)
Vaso-active intestinal peptide (VIP)	Sp.	<30 pmol/l	Raised levels in VIPoma

For key to samples, see footnote to Table 7.1.

Urine assays

Test	Sample	Reference value	Comments
Amino acids	R	Qualitative screen	Fresh sample is necessary
Aminolaevulinate	24 h	0.8–40 µmol/ 24 h	Increased amounts in acute intermittent porphyria — up to 750 µmol/24 h. *NB:* Urine only darkens on standing
Arsenic	24 h	< 0.67 µmol/l	
Ascorbic acid	—	>5 µmol/kg	Bottle contains acid preservative. Collect 2-h urine sample 4 h after giving 700 mg of ascorbic acid orally. If the patient is deficient s/he may take 3 days or more to reach saturation
Bence-Jones protein	EMU	Absence or presence	Presence suggests multiple myeloma, renal damage, macroglobulinaemia
Beta-2-microglobulin	R	5–370 µg/l	
Bile pigments	R	—	Assessable by urinalysis. Urobilinogen — raised in haemolytic anaemia. Reduced or absent in biliary obstruction. Bilirubin appears early in hepatocellular disease and cholestasis
Cadmium	24 h	230–750 nmol/l	
Calcium	24 h	2.7–8.0 mmol/ 24 h	Raised in hypercalcaemia, acromegaly and idiopathic hypercalciuria
Catecholamines	24 h	Check with laboratory	Bottle contains acid preservative. Results comprise dopamine, adrenaline and noradrenaline. See HMMA
Chloride	24 h	100–250 mmol/ 24 h	

Urine assays (*continued*)

Test	Sample	Reference value	Comments
Copper	24 h	0.2–1.0 μmol/ 24 h	Raised in hepatolenticular degeneration (Wilson's disease). Levels rise further during penicillamine treatment
Coproporphyrins	24 h	50–350 nmol	Protect sample from light. Levels raised in porphyria variegata, hereditary coproporphyria, lead poisoning
Cortisol	24 h	100–300 nmol/ 24 h	If result is < 330 nmol/24 h in males or < 280 nmol/24 h in females: patient is unlikely to have Cushing's syndrome
Creatine	24 h	0–400 μmol/24 h (0–50 mg/24 h)	Increased in childhood, pregnancy and muscle disorders
Creatinine	24 h	9–17 mmol/24 h	See under Urine assays
Creatinine clearance	24 h	90–120 ml/min	See under Biochemical equations
Cystine	R 24 h	Negative 0.04–0.45 mmol/24 h	Levels raised along with those of arginine, lysine, and ornithine, in cystinuria. Associated with renal calculi
Glucose	R	Negative	See under Diagnosis of diabetes (Chapter 6)
5HIAA	24 h	< 70 μmol/24 h	5HIAA is a degradation product of serotonin. Levels are raised greatly in patients with secondary deposits from carcinoid tumours
HMMA	24 h	15–50 μmol/24 h	VMA is a degradation product of catecholamines present in raised amounts in patients with phaeochromocytoma or other neuroendocrine tumours. Container contains acid. Special diet required — contact dietitian
Lead	24 h	< 400 nmol/24 h	Levels raised in lead poisoning

Urine assays (*continued*)

Test	Sample	Reference value	Comments
Magnesium	24 h	3.0–6.0 mmol/24 h	
Mercury	24 h	< 50 nmol/24 h	
Metanephrines	24 h	Check with laboratory	
Osmolality	R	40–1400 mosmol/kg	EMU results usually > 600 mosmol/kg. Check age-adjusted range
Oxalate	24 h	0.1–0.4 mmol/24 h	Acid container needed. Levels raised in primary congenital hyperoxaluria
Phosphate	24 h	15–50 mmol/24 h	Acid container needed. Raised in hyperparathyroidism
Porphobilinogen	R 24 h	Not detected 1–10 µmol/24 h	Fresh sample required, protect from sunlight. Raised to over 500 µmol/24 h in acute intermittent porphyria
Porphyrin	R 24 h	Not detected 0–35 nmol/24 h	Fresh sample required, protect from sunlight. Raised in congenital porphyria (type 1) and in symptomatic hepatic porphyria. There may also be a rise in acute porphyria, porphyria variegata and hereditary coproporphyria
Potassium	24 h	40–120 mmol/24 h	High in diuretic therapy
Protein	24 h	< 0.16 g/24 h	
Sodium	24 h	50–250 mmol/l	Varies with intake. Raised in chronic nephritis and Addison's disease
Specific gravity	R	1016–1022	High in DM. Low in DI. Renal damage due to hypercalcaemic and hypokalaemic renal failure
Urate	24 h	1.5–5.0 mmol/24 h	Levels affected by purine content of diet
Urea	24 h	250–500 mmol/24 h	
Urobilinogen	24 h	< 6.7 µmol/24 h	

Urine assays (*continued*)

Test	Sample	Reference value	Comments
VMA			See HMMA
Zinc	24 h	3–15 µmol/24 h	

For key to samples, see footnote to Table 7.1.

Immunology tests

Test	Sample	Comments
Anti-acetylcholine receptor Ab	C	High in myaesthenia gravis in 80% of cases
Adrenal cell Ab	C	Present in Addison's disease
Anti-cardiolipin Ab (lupus anticoagulant)	C	An anti-phospholipid Ab. Prolongs coagulation tests but paradoxically associated with high risk of arterial or venous thrombosis. Also results in a false positive in syphilis
Anti-centromere Ab	C	Found in the CREST syndrome
Anti-DNA Ab	C	Double- or single-stranded DNA Ab described. Double-stranded specific for SLE. Single-stranded not specific
Anti-neutrophil cytoplasmic Ab	C	Found in Wegner's granulomatosis, PAN
Anti-glomerular basement membrane Ab	C	Found in Goodpasture's syndrome
Anti-Jo1 Ab	C	Found in polymyositis
Anti-La Ab	C	Found in primary Sjögren's syndrome, mild SLE
Anti-nuclear factor	C	Non-specific anti-nuclear Ab
Anti-ribonuclear Ab	C	Found in mixed connective tissue disease
Anti-Ro Ab	C	Found in primary Sjögren's syndrome. (Not associated with other auto-immune disease.)
Anti-Scl 70 Ab	C	Found in progressive cases of scleroderma
Anti-Sm Ab	C	Found in 35% of SLE cases
C-reactive protein		See under Chemical pathology tests
C1 esterase inhibitor	C	Needs to be transferred to laboratory immediately. Normals should have 100% activity results. 15% less than normal suggests deficiency, which may be required or inherited, resulting in angioedema
Complement C3/C4	C	Reference values: C3 0.80–1.5 g/l C4 0.15–0.35 g/l Transfer to laboratory immediately. Levels low in SLE. Can be useful in following progress of disease

Immunology tests (*continued*)

Test	Sample	Comments
Extractable nuclear Ag	C	Reference value: titre < 10 Present in Raynaud's syndrome, SLE, Sjögren's syndrome, RA
HLA B27	C or EDTA	Associated with ankylosing spondylitis, Reiter's disease, juvenile chronic polyarthritis, IBD, 5% of normal people
Immunoglobulins	C	See under Chemical pathology tests
Insulin Ab	C	Associated with auto-immune hypoglycaemia, type 1 diabetes (monoclonal), insulin administration (polyclonal). Detected by immuno-assay
Intrinsic factor Ab	C	Found in 50% of patients with PA Type 1 — inhibits binding of intrinsic factor to B_{12} Type 2 — inhibits binding of B_{12}/intrinsic factor complex to receptor site in ileum
Islet cell Ab	C	Found in type 1 DM, often transiently
Liver/kidney microsomal Ab	C	May be found in chronic active hepatitis: useful if other Ab negative
Mitochondrial Ab	C	Found in primary biliary cirrhosis
Ovarian Ab	C	Found in primary ovarian failure
Parietal cell Ab	C	Found in PA, chronic atrophic gastritis, auto-immune endocrinopathies, thyroid disease
RA latex	C	Reference value: 0–60 iu/ml. Very high in RA, Sjögren's syndrome. High in SLE, polymyositis, liver disease
Rose–Waller tests (RA)	C	Reference value: < 32. High in 75% of adults with RA, but rheumatoid factor is present in many adults without RA
Smooth muscle Ab	C	Chronic active hepatitis
Thyroglobulin Ab	C	May be positive in hyperthyroidism, auto-immune thyroiditis
Thyroid microsomal Ab	C	Primary hypothyroidism

Ab = antibody; Ag = antigen; C = clotted.

Serology tests

Test	Sample	Comments
ASO titre	C	Reference value: check with laboratory. High in haemolytic streptococcal infection, rheumatic fever etc.
Aspergillus precipitins	C	Ab usually absent in healthy individuals. Strongly positive in patients with aspergilloma. Weakly positive in allergic bronchopulmonary aspergillosis
Brucella agglutination	C	Reference value: > 1 : 60. A single titre > 1 : 60 is suggestive of brucellosis. An agglutination test which demonstrates a fourfold or greater rise in titre over a 4 week period is highly suggestive of brucellosis. Elevated serum IgG is detected by extraction with 2-mercapto-ethanol — this is evidence of current or recent infection. A negative 2-mercapto-ethanol test excludes chronic infection
Coccidioides Ab	C	Highly specific latex agglutination and precipitin tests are available
	CSF	A positive result is diagnostic of coccidioides meningitis
Cryptococcal Ab	Biopsy	Demonstrate the organisms in appropriately stained tissue sections
	CSF	A positive latex cryptococcal agglutination test is diagnostic of cryptococcosis
Echinococcus Ab	C	May be positive in most cases of hydatid disease unless the patient has a single intact cyst. Casoni skin test no longer used because of lack of specificity
Entamoeba FAT	C	Titre > 1 : 200 is significant. Positive in 90% of cases of liver abscess; 75% with active colitis; low titre if asymptomatic. A negative result should be obtained before giving steroids in a patient with ulcerative colitis
FTA		See syphilis
Filarial FAT	C	Serological tests are not specific
Giardiasis	C	Look for raised specific IgG or IgM in acute infections
Gonococcus CFT	C	Serological tests are generally not thought to be useful

Serology tests (*continued*)

Test	Sample	Comments
Hepatitis A virus Ab	C	Presence of Ab indicates immunity. Diagnosis by presence of IgM class Ab or fourfold rise in serial samples of IgG. Detectable for up to 60 days after onset of symptoms
Hepatitis B virus	C	**1** Antigens. HBsAg is indicative of hepatitis B infection and appears in blood from approximately 6 weeks to 3 months after inoculation. It may indicate present or chronic infection or carrier status. HBcAg is not found in the serum. HBeAg correlates with viral replication and infectivity (hepatitis B DNA is a more specific marker) **2** Antibodies. Anti-HBsAg is indicative of past hepatitis B infection or immunisation. Appears several months after infection. Anti-HBcAg is present during infection and persists after viral clearance. IgM Anti-HBcAg is mainly present during acute infection and is the first Ab to appear. Anti-HBeAg indicates a state of inactivity with absent viral replication and low infectivity
Hepatitis C Ab	C	Anti-HCVAb: a recently developed ELISA test is available which is not wholly specific. More specific tests will soon be developed. Current test takes 3–6 months to appear following acute infection and may persist for years
Hepatitis E Ab	C	An epidemic form of non-A–non-B hepatitis: a diagnostic test likely to be available in the near future
Histoplasma Ab CFT	C	Titre > 1 : 32 significant. Ab develops within 3 weeks of onset
Legionella Ab	C .	Titres > 1 : 256 are diagnostic; alternatively look for a fourfold rising titre. Indirect immunofluorescence used

Serology tests (*continued*)

Test	Sample	Comments
Leptospiral Ab (CFT/agglutination)	C	Specific IgM Ab appears by the end of the first week. If positive do a Schueffner test which a figure of > 1 : 100 is significant
Listeria Ab	C	Diagnosis generally made by blood or CSF culture
Lyme disease	C	Specific IgM *Borrelia burgdorferi* Ab can be detected
Mycoplasma	C	Look for a fourfold rising titre
Syphilis	C	FTA-ABS: remains positive for life even after treatment. TPHA: positive in 90% of patients with primary infection and *all* patients with latent and late syphilis. TPI: most specific but rarely used, remains positive for years after successful treatment. VDRL cardiolipin Ag test: positive within 3–4 weeks after infection. Negative by 6 months after treatment, but also if untreated. There are many causes of a false positive VDRL: yaws hepatitis, infectious mononucleosis, mycoplasma infections
Toxocara Ab	C	Detection by ELISA
Toxoplasma Ab	C	Sabin–Feldman dye test: measure of IgG IgM-immunofluorescent Ab: titres rise early and fall rapidly, therefore useful in acute infection. Indirect immunofluorescence and indirect haemagglutination; raised levels common in the general population — therefore only a rising titre is suggestive of infection
Typhoid		See Widal agglutination test
VDRL		See syphilis
Widal (agglutination test)	C	Titres > 1 : 80 to H and O Ag is significant. Measures serum agglutinins against the O and H Ag, a fourfold increase in titre in sequential blood samples is suggestive of *Salmonella typhi* infection (but unreliable in vaccinated patients). A titre of 80 to both H and O Ag suggests active infection in an unvaccinated patient living in an area where typhoid is not endemic

Serology tests (*continued*)

Test	Sample	Comments
Weil–Felix Proteus	C	Being replaced by CFT. This is a serological agglutination test for rickettsial infection (typhus, Q fever, etc.)
Yersinia Ab	C	Ab detected by fluorescent Ab staining

Note: the variety of available immuological tests is rapidly increasing. It is important to note that:

1 All require clotted blood.

2 Most are only significant if serial samples are taken to look for a change or very high titres are found initially.

3 All need specialist interpretation because the significance depends on levels, history and technique.

For key to samples, see footnote to Table 7.1.

Ab = antibody; Ag = antigen; FAT = fluorescent antibody technique; CFT = complement fixation test; FTA-ABS = fluorescent treponemal antibody-absorption (test); HBcAg = hepatitis B core antigen; HBsAg = hepatitis B surface antigen; HBeAg = hepatitis B 'e' antigen; HCVAb = hepatitis C virus antibody; TPHA = *Treponema pallidum* haemagglutination assay; TPI = *Treponema pallidum* immobilisation.

Microbiology tests

Test	Sample	Comments
Actinomycosis	Pus	Infection may result in a chronic granulomatous inflammation
Adenovirus		Send swab from throat or conjunctiva, or faeces or paired sera
Amoebic dysentery	Faeces	Trophozoites only found in faeces if blood is present in the stool
Chlamydia A Ag detection **1** Neonatal conjunctivitis **2** Cervicitis **3** Urethritis		Depends on site of infection (a) Cytology, i.e. direct demonstration with Giemsa staining (b) Cell culture Cell culture Cell culture
Clostridium difficile	Faeces	Examine for toxin and organism
CSF		See under Cerebrospinal fluid changes in meningitis
Diphtheria		Nose and throat swab necessary. *Corynebacterium diphtheriae* grows rapidly and faster than other upper respiratory bacteria in Loeffler's medium. These bacteria are commensals and only cause disease opportunistically
Legionella	Sputum	Culture takes up to 3 weeks. See under Serology tests
Leptospira agglutination	CSF Blood Urine	*Leptospira icterohaemorrhagica* may be cultured from the blood or CSF during week 1; from urine during weeks 2–4. See under Serology tests
Tuberculosis	EMU × 3	Culture reports may take 6–8 weeks. Obtain Ziehl-Nielsen stain initially
Typhoid	Blood Faeces Urine	Blood cultures: 80% positive in week 1; 30% positive in week 3. Urine culture positive in week 2 Stool culture positive in weeks 2-4. See under Serology tests

EMU = early morning urine

Oncology tests

Test	Sample	Reference value	Comments
Acid phosphatase	C	Total < 4 iu/l Prostatic: < 1.6 iu/l	Haemolysis interferes with assay. Total level raised in Paget's disease; prostatic level raised in disseminated prostatic cancer. Note that PSA is now preferred where available
Alkaline phosphatase isoenzymes	C		Bone, liver, gut, placenta (found in cancer of the lung, breast, uterus, ovary, myelomatosis & malignant lymphoma)
Alpha fetoprotein	C	< 10 ku/l	Can be used to monitor hepatocellular cancer, gonadal teratoma, choriocarcinoma
Ca-125	C	< 30 iu/ml	Raised in ovarian cancer and serosal disease (e.g. peritoneal metastases). May be used to assess treatment
Ca-15-3	C	< 30 iu/ml	Raised in breast cancer. May be used to assess treatment
Ca-19-9	C	< 30 iu/ml	Raised in pancreatic, colonic, rectal or gastric cancer. May be used to assess treatment
CEA	C	< 10 μg/l	Monitoring colorectal cancer. Levels over 20 μg/l may be diagnostic. Useful in diagnosing a recurrence
HCG	C	< 15 iu/l	Useful in monitoring treatment of choriocarcinoma & gonadal carcinoma
PSA	C	< 4 μg/l	High in prostatic cancer and benign prostatic hypertrophy — significant false negative level. Used for assessing treatment as well as diagnosis

Ca = carbohydrate antigens.
Samples: C = clotted; CSF = cerebrospinal fluid; EMU = early morning urine.

Cerebrospinal fluid changes in meningitis

	Normal	Viral	Pyogenic	TB
Appearance	Clear	Clear/turbid	Turbid/purulent	Turbid/viscous
Mononuclear cells (per mm^3)	< 5	10–100	< 50	100–300
Polymorph cells	Nil	Nil	200–3000	0–200
Protein (g/l)	0.2–0.4	0.4–0.8	0.5–2.0	0.5–3.0
Glucose (relative to blood glucose)	$> \frac{1}{2}$	$> \frac{1}{2}$	$< \frac{1}{3}$	$< \frac{1}{3}$

Dynamic tests

For information on the indications and interpretation of the following tests, we suggest you consult Zilva, J., Pannall, P. and Mayne, P., *Clinical Chemistry in Diagnosis and Treatment*, Fifth edn, Hodder and Stoughton.

Adrenopituitary function tests

Plasma cortisol
See Endocrinology tests section (above).

Twenty-four hour urinary cortisol
See Urine assays section (above).

Dexamethasone suppression test
Use: for diagnosis of Cushing's syndrome — is there a cranial or peripheral cause?

Method
1 Overnight test
   (a) Measure basal plasma cortisol levels at 0900 h on day 1;
   (b) Give 2 mg dexamethasone at 2300 h on day 1;
   (c) Plasma cortisol levels are measured at 0900 h on day 2.

2 High dose test
   (a) Measure basal plasma cortisol level at 0900 h;
   (b) Give 2 mg dexamethasone po 6 hourly for 2 days, starting at 0900 h on day 1;
   (c) At 0900 h on day 3 measure plasma cortisol.

Interpretation

In pituitary-dependent Cushing's syndrome, plasma cortisol levels after dexamethasone are often less than 50% of the basal level. In other aetiologies this degree of suppression does not occur and the postdexamethasone levels are greater than 50% basal. (See also 24 h urinary cortisol assessment in Urine assays section above.)

Short tetracosactrin test (Synacthen/ACTH test)

Use

Assessment of adrenocortical function.

Method

Perform test in the morning.
1 Rest patient in comfortable position.
2 Insert green (21 G) butterfly for IV access and flush with heparinised saline.
3 Wait 15–30 min to allow hormone levels to return to basal and take 5 ml clotted blood through the butterfly for basal cortisol assessment (discard first 3 ml).
4 Dissolve 250 µg of tetracosactrin in 1 ml sterile water and give IM.
5 After 30 and 60 min take blood for cortisol estimation.

Interpretation

Normally plasma cortisol increases by at least 220 nmol/l to a level of at least 550 nmol/l. Failure to do so suggests Addison's disease. If cortisol levels fail to rise more than 10% above basal levels this also suggests Addison's disease.

If the results are abnormal repeat the assays after a 3 day course of tetracosactrin 1 mg IM daily. If still abnormal this points to adrenal rather than cortical insufficiency.

Combined pituitary stimulation test

This is contra-indicated in those patients with ischaemic heart disease, epilepsy or severe hypopituitarism — check that the patient has a normal ECG and a plasma cortisol result greater than 150 nmol/l before proceeding.

This is a dangerous procedure and a doctor should be present throughout — a syringe loaded with 50 ml of 50% glucose for IV administration and 200 mg of hydrocortisone should be available.

At the end of the test give the patient something substantial to eat.

Use

Assessment of pituitary function in response to the administration of TRH and GnRH and in response to stress (in the form of hypoglycaemia).

Method

1 Insert green (21 G) butterfly and flush with heparinised saline.

2 Prepare six clotted blood bottles and six fluoride oxalate bottles with the patient's name and the time that the sample was taken.

3 Wait 30 min after inserting the butterfly and then take basal clotted and fluoride oxalate samples (discard first 3 ml from the line).

4 Inject 200 μg of TRH, 100 μg of GnRH and a dose of soluble insulin. Depending on the patient's condition, this is usually 0.15 units of insulin per kilogram of body weight:

Patient wt (kg)	Insulin dose (u)
50	7.5
60	9.0
70	10.5
80	12.0
90	13.5
100	15.0

If hypofunction is thought to be probable or the patient has previously had a very low fasting glucose give 0.05–0.1 units of insulin per kilogram of body weight:

Patient wt (kg)	Insulin dose (u)
50	2.5–5.0
60	3.0–6.0
70	3.5–7.0
80	4.0–8.0
90	4.5–9.0
100	5.0–10.0

If the patient is cushingoid, acromegalic or obese give 0.2–0.4 units of insulin per kilogram of body weight:

Patient wt (kg)	Insulin dose (u)
50	10–20
60	12–24
70	14–28
80	16–32
90	18–36
100	20–40

5 Take blood samples at 30, 45, 60, 90 and 120 min after hormone administration (keep samples in the fridge until they are delivered to the laboratory). Assay glucose, GH, FSH, LH, TSH, prolactin and cortisol at each time.

For significant stress to have been imposed on the adreno-pituitary system the blood glucose should fall below 2.2 mmol/l and the patient should be symptomatic for this induced hypoglycaemia (hungry, sweaty, altered behaviour, tachy-cardic). If the patient does become symptomatic, check the ward glucose level and if very low (less than 2.2 mmol/l) give 50 ml of 50% glucose IV. This does not interfere with the test because adequate stress has been achieved.

Interpretation
If sufficient stress has been imposed:
GH level should rise over 20 mU/l.
TSH should rise by at least 2 mU/l.
Plasma cortisol should rise by more than 200 nmol/l to a level over 550 nmol/l.

Check the expected rise of prolactin and the gonadotrophins with your laboratory.

Insulin suppression test for growth hormone reserve
The protocol and precautions for this test are the same as those outlined for a combined pituitary function test *except* that you only administer insulin.

If sufficient stress is produced the GH level should rise over 20 mU/l.

Glucose suppression test

Use
Diagnosis of acromegaly/gigantism.

Method
1 Patient should be fasted overnight.
2 Insert green (21 G) butterfly and flush with heparinised saline.
3 Wait at least 30 min.
4 Take basal samples for glucose and GH estimation (discard first 3 ml).

5 Give patient 75 g of glucose dissolved in 250–300 ml of water, po — to drink over 4 min.

6 Take further blood samples for glucose and GH at 30, 60, 90 and 120 min after glucose ingestion.

Interpretation

In normals GH levels should fall to less than 5 mU/l. In those with acromegaly/gigantism this fails to happen.

NB: Many laboratories have developed a more convenient method of administering a glucose load. Some use Lucozade whilst others prefer Fortical diluted with water — check with your laboratory.

Water deprivation test

Use

Differentiation between psychogenic polydypsia and DI.

Method

NB: This test should not be performed on patients who are already dehydrated (if there is low urine osmolality with high inappropriate plasma osmolality then a diagnosis of DI has already been made).

Patients should be observed throughout and if they become distressed then collect samples and terminate the test. The object is to assess whether a patient with polyuria is able to concentrate his or her urine when deprived of fluid intake. If s/he is unable to do so, this suggests a deficiency of ADH (cranial DI) or renal resistance to ADH (nephrogenic DI).

1 The patient should be nil by mouth for a length of time dependent on the severity of the polyuria. If the patient is passing in excess of 6 litres of urine per 24 h it would be dangerous to keep him or her NBM for 13 h as suggested in some protocols. Ask for advice from your chemical pathology department on how long to keep the patient NBM. Whatever time period is deemed suitable, do not keep the patient NBM if his or her weight drops more than 3% (indicating a significant loss of fluid).

2 After this suitable period, ask the patient to void the bladder and take a blood sample. Then check the urinary and plasma osmolality.

- If urine osmolality is more than 850 mmol/kg, terminate the test since DI has been excluded.
- If urine osmolality is less than 850 mmol/kg, if the plasma osmolality is normal, and the patient's weight has not dropped by more than 3%, measure the urine and plasma osmolality at 1 h intervals for 2 h.

Interpretation

If the patient's kidneys are unable to concentrate the urine in the face of a normal or raised plasma osmolality you have proof of impaired concentrating ability. This may be due to a relative lack of ADH or peripheral resistance.

If three consecutive urine samples show a low osmolality and there is no rise in consecutive samples, give 4 μg DDAVP or 5 u Pitressin (ADH) IM and take further hourly urine and plasma samples for osmolality. If lack of ADH is the problem, administration of synthetic ADH should lead to a rise in urine osmolality. If the patient has nephrogenic DI no improvement will be found.

Never continue if the patient's weight drops more than 3% from basal *at any stage*.

Gastrointestinal tests

Pentagastrin stimulation test

Use

Assessment of gastric acid production under basal conditions and in response to maximal stimulation by pentagastrin. Note that the patient must have been off H_2-blockers or omeprazole for more than 3 days.

Method

1 Following an overnight fast, pass a nasogastric tube and aspirate all 'resting juices'.

2 After a further half-hour aspirate all 'basal' juices.

3 Give 6 µg/kg body weight pentagastrin SC or IM:

Patient wt (kg)	Pentagastrin dose (µg)
50	300
60	360
70	420
80	480
90	540
100	600

4 Take four aspirate samples at 15 min intervals and label samples appropriately (aspiration of all of the stomach contents is important).

Interpretation

The volume, pH and acid content of each sample will be analysed. The normal basal acid output is less than 5 mmol/h. The normal peak acid output, calculated from the peak 30 min secretion, is:

• Males: less than 30 mmol/h
• Females: less than 25 mmol/h

If the pH does not drop below 3.5 the patient is described as 'pentagastrin fast'; this is typical of pernicious anaemia. A high basal output with no further response to stimulation suggests the Zollinger–Ellison syndrome.

There are newer alternatives to this technique which include 'sham eating' or postprandial urine alkalisation tests — check with your laboratory.

Xylose absorption test

NB: Renal failure and generalised oedema may invalidate this test. It is non-specific and therefore rarely helpful except when serious doubt exists as to the cause of malabsorption.

Use
Assessment of GI absorption.

Method
1 Fast patient overnight.
2 Void bladder and administer 5 g of xylose in 250 ml of water orally. After a further hour up to 250 ml of water/hour may be given to encourage urine flow.
3 Collect all urine passed over the next 2 h into the same container ('Bottle 1'). Void bladder at the end of this 2 h period into Bottle 1.
4 Collect all urine over the next 3 h into a second container (Bottle 2) including that passed at the end of this period.

Interpretation
The excretion of 8.0–16 mmol xylose in the 5 h after intake is normal, 4.6–11 mmol being excreted in the first 2 h.
Fifty per cent or more of the total excretion should occur in the first 2 h.
In mild intestinal malabsorption the 5 h excretion may be normal but the 2 h level with be reduced.
In severe intestinal malabsorption all figures may be reduced.
Pancreatic insufficiency does not interfere with this test.

Other tests

Ammonium chloride load test

Use
Assessment of congenital or acquired RTA.

NB: If any urine pH is less than 5.3, RTA is excluded.

Method
1 Overnight fast.
2 Give ammonium chloride 0.1 g/kg body weight orally next morning:

Patient wt (kg)	Dose of ammonium chloride (g)
50	5
60	6
70	7
80	8
90	9
100	10

3 Void bladder at 3 h and discard. Then void bladder at 4, 5 and 6 h. Seal the containers, ensure that they are correctly labelled and transfer to the laboratory immediately.
4 Take blood for plasma bicarbonate at hour 5.

Interpretation
At least one urine sample should have a pH of less than 5.3. In RTA this fails to occur.

Thyroid function tests
The interpretation of thyroid function tests has become easier with the use of more sensitive assay techniques. Recently developed assays for TSH for example can now distinguish between normal subjects (0.5–2.9 mU/l) and values found in hyperthyroid individuals which are significantly reduced (< 0.1 mU/l). This has reduced the indications for doing a TRH test.

If the TSH is normal, this excludes hyperthyroidism and there is no need to proceed to a TRH test.

This test may be useful in proving that a patient with

borderline TSH levels and borderline low T4 levels is hypothyroid. If so they will show a raised TSH level 20 min after TRH administration with a persistently raised level at 60 min. In normals, the 20 min result is raised but the 60 min level has fallen to normal.

TRH test

1 Give 200 µg TRH IV.
2 Assay blood TSH levels at 20 and 60 min.

Glucose tolerance test

Use

The WHO criteria for diagnosis of DM are outlined above in the Chemical pathology tests section under Glucose.

Method

1 Overnight fast.
2 Take fasting sample for plasma glucose.
3 Give 75 g of oral glucose with 250–300 ml of water — to drink over 4 min.
4 Take a sample for plasma glucose at 2 h.

Interpretation

If the fasting plasma level is more than 7.8 mmol/l, DM is diagnosed.

If the fasting plasma level is less than 7.8 mmol/l and the 2 h level is between 7.8 and 11.1 mmol/l, impaired glucose tolerance is diagnosed.

If the 2 h plasma level is more than 11.1 mmol/l, DM is indicated.

If the 2 h plasma level is less than 7.8 mmol/l, this is a normal result.

NB: many laboratories have developed a more convenient method of administering a glucose load. Some use Lucozade whilst others prefer Fortical diluted with water — check with your laboratory.

Biochemical equations

Anion gap
(Na + K) – (Cl + HCO$_3$).
Normal = 4 – 17 mmol
The gap is made up of phosphate, sulphate, protein, pyruvate, lactate and other ions.
- *High*: diabetic keto-acidosis, renal failure, lactic acidosis, methanol or salicylate ingestion, hepatic failure.
- *Low*: hypoalbuminaemia, liver disease, multiple myeloma.

Corrected calcium
There are many different equations for calculating the 'corrected calcium' result to account for raised or reduced albumin levels. The number of equations is testimony to the fact that at best all of them are estimations because the relationship between ionised calcium and albumin levels is complex. Many laboratories now report corrected or ionised calcium results.

A useful approximation is as follows:

For every 1 g/l that the albumin result is more than 40 g/l, subtract 0.02 to the calcium result.

For every 1 g/l that the albumin result is less than 40 g/l, add 0.02 from the calcium result.

Or — use the following equation:

$$\text{Corrected Ca}^{++} = (\text{total Ca}^{++} + 1) - (0.25 \times \text{albumin})$$

Creatinine clearance

$$\text{Creatinine clearance (ml/min)} = \frac{\text{Urinary creatinine} \times \text{urine volume (ml)}}{\text{Plasma creatinine} \times \text{length of collection (min)}}$$

NB: The plasma creatinine must be measured during the 24 h urine collection period.

It is possible to calculate an approximate creatinine clearance value without the need to do a 24 h urine collection by use of the following formulae:

Males

$$\text{Creatinine clearance} \approx \frac{1.23 \times (140 - \text{age}) \times \text{wt (kg)}}{\text{Creatinine (μmol/l)}}$$

Females

$$\text{Creatinine clearance} \approx \frac{1.04 \times (140 - \text{age}) \times \text{wt (kg)}}{\text{Creatinine (μmol/l)}}$$

Plasma osmolality (mosmol/kg)

$$\approx 2\,(Na^+ K^+) + \text{urea} + \text{glucose}$$

Low density lipoprotein cholesterol (Friedwald's equation)

$$\text{Total cholesterol} - \frac{TG}{2.2} - HDL$$

Globulins

Total protein – albumin

Indirect bilirubin

Total bilirubin – direct bilirubin

Index